LIFE ISN'T FAIR
BUT
LIFE IS GOOD

TAMMY WONDRA

WESTBOW
P R E S S®
A DIVISION OF THOMAS NELSON
& ZONDERVAN

WestBow Press books may be ordered through booksellers or by contacting:

WestBow Press
A Division of Thomas Nelson & Zondervan
1663 Liberty Drive
Bloomington, IN 47403
www.westbowpress.com
844-714-3454

Scripture quotations taken from The Holy Bible, New International Version® NIV® Copyright © 1973 1978 1984 2011 by Biblica, Inc. TM. Used by permission. All rights reserved worldwide.

Interior Image Credit: Holly Ellefson (introduction picture, picture at end of book, author picture), Patty Wondra (wedding picture)

ISBN: 978-1-6642-4743-7 (sc)
ISBN: 978-1-6642-4742-0 (hc)
ISBN: 978-1-6642-4744-4 (e)

Library of Congress Control Number: 2021921027

Print information available on the last page.

WestBow Press rev. date: 10/18/2021

BOOK DEDICATION

This book is dedicated to the two people who walked this journey with me.

To my husband, Mark, who gave me the blessed gift of love and commitment. Our 18 years together weren't always easy, but together we made it. It was an honor being your wife, and I look forward to seeing you again in Heaven.

To my daughter, Hannah, who brings me such joy and love every single day. You are a precious gift from God, and I'm blessed that He chose me to raise you. You were worth the journey, and I'm so grateful for you and the happiness you bring. I'm proud to be your mom.

Hi there! I'm Tammy. I'm so excited and honored you picked up my book. Thank you. I pray my story touches you and inspires you.

God is good all the time!

Jeremiah 29:11 "For I know the plans I have for you," declares the Lord, "plans to prosper you and not to harm you, plans to give you hope and a future."

ACKNOWLEDGMENTS

There are many people who have helped contribute to this story. Without their love and support, this book wouldn't be possible.

I am incredibly thankful for my amazing parents, Bruce and Patsy Gustafson, my brothers, Aaron and Chad (Ajay), my sister, Danielle (Matt), along with my nieces, Bemnet, Peyton and Adelaide, and my nephews, Tyler, Sam and James. You walked this journey with me from day one and never left my side. Your prayers, love, and support guided me through the toughest and happiest parts of my life. I'm honored to call you my family. I couldn't have made it without you. Your encouragement to fulfill my dream of writing a book means so much to me. I love you with all my heart.

I'm grateful beyond words for my friend, April Wallace. You encouraged me through some of the hardest points of this journey. When I wanted to give up, you wouldn't let me. When I was leaning the wrong way, you turned me the right way, and you never steered me wrong. You are a wonderful "auntie" for Hannah. We chose to give Hannah her middle name in your honor. It means the world to Hannah to share a middle name with you. Your love and support is a beautiful blessing in my life. I love you so much, my dear "sister".

The gift that Scott, Rose, Jamie and Mandi gave when Scott donated his kidney to Mark is a gift that is irreplaceable. You guys gave us a better quality of life and more time together. I always struggle with the perfect words to express how much your sacrificial gift meant to us. Mark cherished the gift of life you gave him. I'm grateful for the relationship Scott and Mark had and the bond our families will always share. I love you guys.

I'm thankful for our medical team of doctors including Dr. Jim Wallace, Dr. David Warden, Dr. Glenn Nickele, Erin Dehn PA-C, Dr. Gurdesh Bedi, Dr. Danielle Redburn, Kelly Schmidt, NP and Dr. Bill Schultz. You became more than just doctors to us. You all are like family. You did what you could to help our family in whatever capacity it took. You are a blessing to your patients!

To the nursing staff of St. Croix Regional Medical Center and St. Croix Hospice, your medical expertise, love, and support helped us during some of our hardest moments. You not only treated us like patients, but like a member of the family. I thank you!

I couldn't have made it without the faith, love, and support of our church families, Trade Lake Baptist Church and Alliance Church of the Valley. There were many times we needed things done, and you never hesitated to help. There were benefits organized for us and even a ramp that was built in just a couple days when we desperately needed it fast. The love of God was evident through the support and love of our church families, and we couldn't have gotten through it without you. Thank you for showing the love of Christ to us.

Thank you to my co-workers at St. Croix Regional Medical Center who provided meals, gift cards, patience, and support when I needed it most. You reminded me time and time again that family always came first and work was second, even if that meant extra work on your shoulders. Thank you for your patience and always being there for me.

The Milberg family went through a horrible family tragedy and their love and support shown to us is a huge blessing, especially as I know they are hurting deeply themselves. Our journeys have been devastating, but they brought us together. I praise God for that. I'm blessed to have you in my life! Kari, you were a big support to Mark. He greatly appreciated you and how you understood him—his fellow TBI warrior.

Our frozen embryo transfer wouldn't have been possible without the selfless, precious gift from my friend, Kami. Because of you, I fulfilled a dream of being pregnant with twins. It's an experience I will cherish forever. I love you!

I'm grateful for the Wondra family who supported us when they did. Seeing your loved one struggle had to be hard. I appreciate you being there for us when you were able to. Thank you to Holly Route for filling in pieces of family history included in this book!

I'm incredibly thankful for my friends, April Wallace, Rachel Riebe, Samara Duncan and Rita Platt, and my mom, for their editing skills and advice. You helped guide and encourage me to expand and stretch my thinking. Your patience and guidance is very appreciated. I'm grateful for your friendship!

Thank you to my friend, Holly Ellefson, for her amazing photography skills and taking gorgeous photos to include in this book. You are amazing!

Most of all, I'm grateful for my Lord and Savior for His trust, love, and guidance through my life. I'm humbled and honored that You have chosen me to walk this path in life in Your honor. I pray my life glorifies You.

PROLOGUE

Dear 20-year-old Tammy,

You may not know me, but I know you. At twenty years of age the future looks uncertain and kind of scary.

To you right now is 1996, but for me it is 2016. Things are vastly different from what you could imagine! I'm twenty years older, and if you saw me on the street you wouldn't even recognize me.

I know you're struggling right now. Remember after you graduated from high school, after being so successful in sports, you were on top of the world? You were ready for college and set to become a veterinarian. You were dreaming of the man you would marry, planning for an amazing marriage, birthing four kids, living your childhood dream of working as a veterinarian and saving the lives of animals. Everything was going to be easy.

You never dreamed you'd be in the position you are now. You are coming to realize college just isn't for you. You are back living at home and working two jobs, praying you'll find your path again. I know you are thinking your life is a mess. You're depressed and wondering how life could get so hard!

What you don't know is that the hardest is yet to come. You can't begin to guess what hurdles you will overcome.

You'll never predict you will meet the man you're going to marry shortly after starting your second job.

You don't know that when you marry him you will hope to be

blessed with five years of marriage before he passes away because of life-threatening health issues.

You can't imagine what your first year of marriage will be like. How you will encounter countless surgeries, dialysis runs, and endless trips to the ER.

You don't know your dream of giving birth to four kids will be such a struggle and an impossibility.

You'll never believe you'll endure eight years of infertility, twelve IUIs (intrauterine inseminations), an IVF (in vitro fertilization) cycle, and two FET (frozen embryo transfer) cycles before you finally turn to adoption.

I'm not telling you this to devastate you. I don't want you to give up because you don't believe you can do it.

I'm here to tell you that you can and you will.

You won't know how strong your husband is until you see how his strength and faith are an inspiration to people all over the world.

You can't guess that your daughter will be brought into this world in a miraculous way best described as a "God thing", and that her story will help others realize miracles really do happen.

You will be shocked how others will be inspired by your marriage and faith and how much your story will touch them.

You don't know that all this will be possible precisely because of your struggles now at age twenty. Your break from college, and your second job, where you meet your husband, will change your life plans completely.

You'll go through more in the next twenty years than most people go through in a lifetime.

Right now, you need to know, you'll be okay. Your faith in God will be stronger, magnified, ten fold by your journey.

Later, you'll get it. You'll feel and know you are the luckiest woman in the world as you hold your sleeping daughter in your arms.

You have a hard road ahead of you. But I promise you, you'll be okay. Just like I know my 60-year-old self would tell me the same thing if she were talking to me now.

I know you'll always be okay, because God is right by your side. Always.

Your story is amazing, and I promise it's worth it.

Hang in there. You're in for a wild ride.

Love,
40-year-old Tammy

CONTENTS

CHAPTER 1

My Early Years

I had my life all planned out. I was going to college to become a veterinarian, marry a farmer, and have four kids, two boys and two girls. Yep, that was how my life was going to be. I was a planner, an organizer and set goals for myself. I wasn't big on surprises. So from the time I was young, I had planned out my life, and I was going to achieve it.

But I didn't mention my plan to God. That might have been a mistake!

I grew up in a healthy, happy Christian family. My dad was a farmer, and my mom was an accountant. I had one sister and two brothers. I thought it was the perfect family and life experience, which was why I wanted the same number of kids and the same type of life experience. My parents did a wonderful job raising us. We learned the value of hard work as we farmed. Our parents provided everything we needed. We didn't have the flashiest stuff, and we certainly struggled plenty of times, but we had everything we needed. And we had each other.

Our family attended Trade Lake Baptist Church from the time I was a baby and throughout my childhood. Our church family became a second family to us. I was baptized when I was twelve. Church was very important to my parents. They faithfully brought us to church on Sunday mornings and kids clubs on Wednesday nights. I'm forever grateful for their influence and how they taught us all to put God first.

In high school, I was a member of the National Honor Society, Future Farmers of America, and band. I was involved in cross country, gymnastics, and track. I had a successful high school sports career. I competed at state in gymnastics three years in a row. I was on television because I was in the top four in Wisconsin on the balance beam. I held all five school records in gymnastics. I held the school and conference record in the 1600 meter run in track. I finished my high school sports career with the Senior Athlete Award, an award given to the top senior athlete during the four years of high school in the graduating class. This was an award that was challenging to get because there were tremendous athletes in our school. It was an award I wanted so badly. When it was announced that I had gotten it, I felt like I had just won an Olympic gold medal.

I loved competing in sports in high school. I was a valuable athlete and people respected athletic authority. I loved the success I had. I set goals for myself, and I achieved them. I graduated with honors. My high school goals and achievements were important to me. While most students look forward to graduating, I didn't. I felt comfortable at school. I was scared to get into the "real world". Everyone knew me at high school. Younger kids looked up to me, and I loved being a role model to them. I felt important. I felt needed and special. I loved knowing people knew me. Who would I be outside of school?

The thought of going to college, where everything would be new and different, was terrifying. But it was reality. I knew that. If I wanted to pursue my dream as a veterinarian, I obviously had to go onto college. So I did. I moved into a dorm room my freshman year and had a kind, friendly roommate. But I was homesick. I craved the comfortable safety of high school, my family, and my hometown. I had gone from being well-known and loved to being a complete stranger to everyone. I didn't participate in any sports because I wanted to concentrate on my studies.

I wasn't adjusting well. I made it through the first semester of college somehow, which was an accomplishment for me. I felt proud I was able to do that. Maybe it would work out after all. Maybe I just needed a little time to refresh myself. I spent Christmas break at home working and felt better. I was back in my comfort zone.

When break was over and the second semester of my freshman year started, I went back to college and my dorm. I quickly began to struggle again. After only a couple weeks, I was more homesick than ever. It was hard to admit I needed a change, but I knew what I had to do. I moved out of the dorms and back home. I decided I would do better living at home and commuting to school.

It felt like a huge step back, and I was ashamed, but I was also blessed to have parents who understood and were supportive. They didn't push me into anything I wasn't ready for. They were very patient. I believe this was a big reason why I didn't give up. I wanted them to be proud of me. I didn't want to let them down. I knew they had been proud of my success in high school, and I wanted that to continue. For the next year, I commuted an hour every day from home to college. It worked better for me. I needed the comfort of home. Even though I felt like I let everyone down, at least I was still going to college. But it wasn't easy.

When I started my sophomore year, I decided to try sports again. Maybe that was what I needed to enjoy my college experience more. I joined the cross country team. Even though I was commuting to college and my class schedule wouldn't allow me to be able to train with them, I could still be on the team. I thought getting back into sports would help with my confidence. Since I was commuting, I trained by myself, which wasn't ideal. I didn't enjoy training alone. I wasn't getting the push and drive I needed to do my best. Even though my cross country team make it to the National Championships, my running times were nowhere near where they were in high school, and I was feeling more dejected than ever. Nothing seemed to be going the way I had planned, no matter what I tried to do.

I started questioning myself. To be a veterinarian, it was going to take a lot of schooling with good grades. I was feeling the pressure. My confidence was shot. I didn't think I would make a good veterinarian and started to question if it was the path for me. It took awhile for me to admit that. After all, I had wanted to be a veterinarian since I was a little girl. Everyone who knew me kept telling me I was meant to be a veterinarian. I didn't want to let everyone down. What were people going to think? How could I let go of my goal when everyone expected it of me? But I also knew that continuing to pursue college without being fully invested in it emotionally and mentally would be a waste of money and time.

After a year and a half of college, I dropped out. It was one of the lowest points of my life. I felt like a loser. What had happened to me? In high school I set goals and achieved them. Now that I was in college, I couldn't achieve any goals. Here I was, twenty years old, living at home, and working as a waitress. I had graduated as one of the top students in my high school class. I knew younger kids looked up to me. I felt like I had let everyone down.

My parents were unfailingly supportive. They said they understood that college wasn't for everyone, and they just wanted me to be happy. If they had forced me to stay in college, I might have spiraled into a depression and not really cared if I succeeded or not. They provided the support I needed. I felt more encouraged, inspired to keep fighting, and find myself. They wanted me to pursue whatever made me most happy. I am forever grateful to my parents.

I knew I didn't want to be a waitress for the rest of my life. I knew being a veterinarian wasn't for me either. I had never thought of pursuing anything else. I was at a crossroad and didn't know which way to turn, which road to take. I had no idea what I was going to do. Should I go this way or that way? What I wanted to do was turn around and go back to high school with my sports and success. To a place where I felt like I was actually doing something for myself. I wanted to go back in time. But I couldn't. I knew I could only go forward.

My parents encouraged me to work for awhile and give myself time to think about what I wanted to do. They said I could live at home and take a break. So that was what I did. I worked full-time as a waitress, but I still had plenty of time on my hands. I wanted to make money to pay for college. So, I took a second job working at a gas station in town. It was just a couple days a week, but it was enough to keep me busy. The more I worked, the better I felt about myself. I was doing something for my future, even if it was just earning money. I saved as much as I could and worked, what felt like, endless hours.

Working endless hours and earning money became a priority. I wasn't practicing my faith as I should have been. Rather than going to church, when I was given the opportunity to work, I chose to work. I admit my priorities were not on the right track. God knew this. He allowed me to experience this because He wanted me to learn to lean on Him. He gave me more than I could handle. I was overwhelmed with anxiety about my future career. What should be my next steps? I didn't know where to turn for answers. I didn't know how to trust God's plan because I felt like I knew the best plan for myself. I learned to lean on my parents and return to people who would take care of me when I couldn't do it alone. This was a powerful lesson God wanted me to learn. I needed to lean on others, but most of all I needed to lean on Him.

A year after leaving college, I contemplated becoming a travel agent. I loved traveling. I loved looking for deals and planning vacations. I thought it would be great to be able to do that for a living. I was worried about getting homesick if I went away to college again. Coincidentally, my brother was a student at a college known nationally for Hospitality and Tourism Management. Serendipitously, he and his friends were looking for another roommate. Suddenly, I had an opportunity to go back to college, study something I was interested in, and I would have a place to live and experience the comfort of living with my brother. It was all coming together. Finally, I was moving forward with my life and I felt proud.

I planned to come home every weekend because I knew I would still struggle with homesickness. I wanted to work when I was home, but I knew I wouldn't be able to keep both my jobs. I had to make a choice. Should I keep my job as a waitress or at the gas station?

To everyone else, this dilemma was a no-brainer. I made twice as much money as a waitress, but my schedule included working until three in the morning. The hours were tough and I wasn't a night owl. I was more of an early bird. My hours at the gas station started early in the morning and ended early in the afternoon. During slow times or when there were no customers in the station, I could work on my college studies. I would also have my afternoons and evenings free to spend with family and friends or just relax.

I wanted to enjoy my life a little more and enjoy this college experience. I hadn't enjoyed my first year of college at all, and I didn't want to repeat that. Since I had taken a break from college, I had been going non-stop, working many hours and working hard. The thought of slowing down and concentrating on my studies sounded good to me. So, I quit my job as a waitress and kept my job at the gas station.

As I started getting ready to leave for college, I was looking forward to it. I wanted to study something I was interested in. I would be living with my brother who I adored and I was comforted by being near him. I had a job with great hours, I felt encouraged, and I was smiling more again. Life was looking up.

Just before I moved back to college, I walked into work, and there was a new employee. We were introduced but we didn't say much to each other the rest of the night (we were both quiet and on the shy side). The first thing this employee said to me after we had been working together for about an hour was, "You're even quieter than I am!"

I just smiled and said, "Yeah, I'm pretty quiet. What would you like to talk about?"

He just shrugged.

And we went back to saying nothing to each other.

Can you say awkward?

Little did I know I had just had my first conversation with my future husband, Mark Wondra.

The two years in college were tough. It was hard work and I was still working on weekends at the gas station. Mark and I were friendly co-workers but nothing more. After I graduated, we became closer friends. We hung out outside of work and slowly grew more comfortable with each other.

CHAPTER 2

GETTING MARRIED

When Mark was four years old, he became very sick. The flu was going around. His parents assumed that was what he had and he would get better. He would only sip small amounts of 7-Up. After a few days, his worried parents realized he wasn't getting any better. They wrapped him up in a blanket and rushed him to the hospital. He spent several weeks there as the doctors tried to figure out what was wrong. Eventually, they informed his parents that he didn't have the flu. He had juvenile diabetes. Juvenile diabetes, also known as type 1 diabetes, is a disease in which the pancreas does not produce insulin that the body needs to control blood sugar levels. Mark's parents were told he would not survive his teen years. The disease causes complications throughout the whole body including the eyes, stomach, feet, hands, heart, and kidneys. In Mark's childhood years, very little was known about juvenile diabetes and the long-term survival rate wasn't good.

Mark, born the sixth of eight children, grew up in the small town of Frederic, Wisconsin. His parents owned the Willow Cove Resort which was on a lake. Their house had five bedrooms and a very small bathroom. There were four cabins that were rented out on the resort. There were a lot of fun things for the kids to do. The previous owner had farmed, so there were buildings on the land to explore. The children went swimming, boating, fishing, ice skating, and sliding on the hills. They loved to play hide-and-seek and scare each other. Mark never let his diabetes get in his way of living his life. He wasn't expected to live long, so he made the most of the time that he had. He never stopped enjoying his life and he disregarded the prediction he would die as an adolescent.

After graduating from high school, Mark went on to trade school. Then he worked at Northland Church Furniture before becoming an inventory control manager at Straus Knitting Mills. He was a hard worker and enjoyed his jobs. He worked until he was forced to go on disability in 2001 due to the complications related to diabetes.

In addition to his professional life, Mark enjoyed hobbies. He was a man of incredible talent. He was quite artistic and drew numerous pieces of art. He also enjoyed working with wood and made beautiful furniture and toys for his loved ones. He loved to build, and it brought him joy to be able to build special gifts for family and friends. Mark also liked golfing and everything related to classic cars. He was very knowledgeable about cars. He loved collecting model cars and had his own car room filled with 400 cars that he had found over the years.

But his biggest joy was being a father. Mark had been married before we met and had two boys. Together we had our daughter. He loved and cherished his three children. It didn't matter how he felt; he was always there for his kids. His faith and family were his priorities in life.

Mark accepted the Lord as his personal Savior and was baptized in August 2009. His strong faith in God gave him strength and hope during his most difficult days. When he was sick or had trouble sleeping because of pain, instead of focusing on his struggles, he took that time to pray and talk to God.

One of Mark's drawings

Not long after I met Mark he told me he had diabetes. I honestly didn't think twice about it. Diabetes has always been part of my extended family. Multiple family members struggled with type 1 or type 2 diabetes. Type 2 is the more common form of diabetes that affects adults and can be caused by family history, obesity, or other causes, whereas type 1 is more common in children and not related to obesity or other causes, but simply genetics. As I was growing up, family get-togethers and birthday parties always consisted of angel food cake, only half of it being frosted so the people with diabetes could have a piece, sugar-free Jell-O, and sugar-free dishes specifically made for them. It was just a part of our family traditions. It didn't phase me at all. I had even seen my grandpa giving himself insulin shots. I remember feeling sorry for the family members who suffered from it. I couldn't imagine a worse life than not being able to eat sugar and having to give yourself shots every day. As a kid, it sounded like a nightmare. What could be worse?

Little did I know that was just the tip of the iceberg in the life of a diabetic. I didn't realize just how much diabetes can affect the whole body until I married Mark and watched firsthand what he went through.

While we were dating, I didn't notice anything different about him. We had a normal dating life. In fact, I often tell people that the only real true "normal" years that we had were our dating years. I wish we could have had more of those "normal" years. Those were the years that Mark was having complications, but he wasn't suffering from the complications. He had energy. He was working. He would call me after work or on his lunch break to see how my day was going. At the time I didn't realize how precious those times were and how years later I would have given anything to have gotten a call from him at work. Soon after we got engaged, it was all about illnesses, doctors, and surgeries.

One day I went over to his house after work. He had had an appointment earlier that day, and I asked him how it had gone. I could tell from the look in his eyes that he had a lot on his mind. He took a deep breath. "Well, it looks like I either need an insulin pump or a kidney transplant."

Whoa, wait a second. A kidney transplant? This was huge! I had only heard of a few people having transplants, and they were on TV as a part of a big news story. That didn't happen to anyone I knew. At the time I thought this was a huge deal. I didn't realize just how common transplants are in this day and age, and I was panicking. This wasn't just a simple health issue anymore.

I asked what Mark was thinking. He didn't like the thought of an insulin pump and having something hanging out of his body all the time, but he was leaning more towards the pump than a kidney transplant.

"Okay, that sounds reasonable. Where do we start? What's the next step?" I asked.

Mark looked at me. "You mean, you still want to be with me?"

I gave him a funny look. "Well, yeah. Nothing's changed."

Truth be told, I was terrified and panicking. I wasn't sure what was going on or how I would deal with this. But I realized at that moment, I really wanted to be with Mark. I loved him, and I could see a future with him. I knew this was not his journey to walk, but our journey to walk.

He took me into his bathroom and taught me all about what happens in the life of a diabetic. A life that I thought I knew but really didn't. It was overwhelming. He showed me how to check his blood sugar, how to draw up insulin into a syringe, and what to do if his sugar was low and he wasn't responding. "This is my life. This is what you're getting yourself into. It's not going to get easier. It's only going to get harder. It's going to get tough. I understand if you don't want to be a part of it, and you want to walk away."

I'd be lying if I said I didn't think about it. Was I really ready for a huge change in my life like this? It would be understandable if I just told Mark I couldn't do it. I wasn't prepared. I wasn't expecting to take something like this on. I was scared out of my mind. I wasn't a nurse. I had no training. I didn't like needles or blood. But if I wanted to be with Mark, it was going to be a part of my daily life.

"Of course I still want to be a part of your life. Nothing has changed." I said as I gave him a hug.

It wasn't long after that I stopped by his house after work. I barely noticed a small box on his table. I was pretty naive and didn't think too much about it. Mark took me into his arms, gave me a big hug and kiss and said, "I'm going out on a limb here…..and I have a feeling the limb is going to break…..but I want you to be with me the rest of my life."

My eyes got wide as I realized what was happening. He was asking me to marry him! I was in shock but didn't show it.

I said, "Yes!"

Later, Mark told me he was taken by surprise when I said yes. Even though I had already told him his diabetic life didn't matter, he thought I would be scared and walk away. The thought of proposing and hearing me say no terrified him. But he loved me so much and couldn't imagine life without me. He told me he was thankful he had gone out on a limb and that it was such a strong one.

This was in November 2000. At that time, Mark was feeling good. We knew that his kidneys were failing due to the diabetic damage to his kidneys, and we had some decisions to make, but he was still working. Things seemed to going well. I had always wanted a Christmas wedding, so we set a date for December 1, 2001.

But within a couple short months, Mark started getting sick really fast. He could hardly get out of bed. He had to stop working. The decision between an insulin pump and a kidney transplant was no longer a choice. We had to start preparing because Mark needed a kidney transplant. We were hoping to get Mark approved quickly for a kidney transplant and skip over dialysis, but Mark was getting sick so fast that we had to start dialysis immediately.

The kidneys' job in the body is to filter the blood of extra waste and fluid and create the urine. When the kidneys aren't working correctly, it can cause a lot of fluid to build up in your body. This can cause someone to have a lot of swelling, can cause breathing trouble, and lead to exhaustion. When the kidneys fail, sometimes the person has to be put on dialysis. It is a treatment that uses a special machine to filter harmful wastes, salt, and excess fluid from your blood that normally the kidneys do. A person has to sit in a chair for three hours a day three days a week. While it is certainly life-saving and needed, it is a hard treatment and tough on the body.

Because Mark was getting so sick, he needed to start dialysis by March 2001. It was stressful for me. I was an emotional wreck. I would cry at the drop of a hat. I wasn't expecting to deal with this so quickly. I wasn't prepared. Everything was moving too fast. If Mark was this sick now, what did it mean for our future? Was there even a future for us? I was working full-time and having to bring Mark to and from dialysis. It was exhausting for both of us.

Because Mark's health was up in the air, we decided to move the wedding up to May 2001. Both of our families were supportive and thought it was wise. Mark's sister was a florist and offered to do the flowers for our wedding. We picked the first weekend in May, which happened to be Mother's Day weekend. This was a very busy time for my sister-in-law. When I asked her if it would still be okay, she simply said, "Anything for you guys." It meant a lot to me that our families were supportive and willing to do anything for us.

Since I wanted a Christmas wedding, our families worked hard for us to put a Christmas-themed wedding together in six weeks. They dug out the artificial Christmas trees, lights, and decorations and decorated the church to make it look like Christmas. There were candles in the windows and even though it was four o'clock in the afternoon in the middle of May, with the smell of freshly mowed green grass outside, we still had a "candlelight" ceremony. It was beautiful. I will forever be grateful to our family and friends for making my "Christmas wedding" a reality.

Our wedding

CHAPTER 3

THE KIDNEY TRANSPLANT

While we were pulling together a wedding on short notice, Mark was being evaluated for a kidney transplant. There were many tests he had to undergo to be approved for the transplant. A transplant surgery is a serious surgery, so tests had to be run to make sure his body could not only survive a transplant surgery, but also be strong enough to recover from it. So far the tests were coming back with good results, and he was close to being cleared for the transplant.

Just two weeks after our wedding, Mark went in for the last test he needed before being cleared for the transplant. This test was a radiological procedure called an angiogram. An angiogram is a procedure that uses a special dye and camera to take pictures of the blood flow in the arteries of the heart. We were hopeful that after months of tests, we would finally be cleared. We were all breathing a sigh of relief. Right before Mark went in for the procedure, I told him, "Just one more. You've got this."

I'll never forget the moment the angiogram was finished. The doctor came into the waiting room and called for me. He led my mom and me from the waiting room into a small, tan room where he sat across from us with a blank look, like he was trying to decide something and trying to find the words. Then he said, "The procedure went well; however, we did find some significant disease."

My heart dropped. "What does that mean?"

"Well, there is plaque in the blood vessels which is causing decreased blood flow. This will need to be fixed before we can go forward with the kidney transplant. It is too much of a risk to perform the surgery with this amount of disease."

At this point, I stopped listening. My stomach dropped. I felt nauseous. I wanted to run out of that room and pretend this wasn't happening. I wanted to rewind time back a few hours to when we had hope, were optimistic about getting the angiogram done and moving forward with the kidney transplant—finally! When I heard more needed to be done before we could go ahead with the transplant, I was devastated. I was fighting tears with a huge lump in my throat. We were so close and yet so far.

Later, my mom explained more to me about what the doctor said. He wasn't sure what they would do to fix the blockages. The blockages weren't really bad enough to do a bypass surgery but they were significant enough that doing an angioplasty (putting in stents) may not work. An angioplasty has a limited period of recovery whereas a bypass surgery requires at least six weeks of recovery, weeks of cardiac rehabilitation, and another assessment before being cleared again for the transplant. The doctor needed to discuss options with the rest of the team of doctors to decide what would be the best for Mark.

Needless to say, we were hoping and praying that they would decide to do the angioplasty and the stents, so we could move forward faster. When we were told Mark would need to undergo the bypass surgery, we were heartbroken.

The doctors tried their best to encourage us. They told us the bypass surgery was actually the hardest of the surgeries between the bypass and the kidney transplant. Having the kidney transplant and a new working kidney would make Mark feel better and the recovery for the transplant surgery would be much easier. If we could get through the bypass surgery, we would get through the toughest part. I sincerely appreciate how they did their best to keep us optimistic. At that time we needed hope and encouragement. We needed to know things would be getting better and this was just a bump in the road.

In August 2001, Mark underwent a triple bypass open heart surgery to open up the blood flow to his heart. He did really well. Even though he still was receiving dialysis he continued to work on rehabilitation. When he was healed enough we were given the "green light". Finally we were on our way, once again. We were back on the journey to a kidney transplant and breathing a sigh of relief.

Little did we know we were in for more heartache.

While Mark was recovering and completing his cardiac rehabilitation, the search for a living kidney donor continued. This wasn't easy, and we were faced with alternating hope and heartache. The transplant almost didn't happen.

In order to be considered to donate a kidney, both the donor and the recipient need to have the same blood type. There are four different blood types: A, AB, B, and O. Mark had type O blood. This meant he could only receive a kidney from someone with type O blood. O is considered to be "universal" which means this blood type can be used with any other blood type. For example, someone with type A blood could receive a kidney from someone with type A blood or type O blood. In other words, blood types with the exception of type O can receive from that blood type plus O, thereby doubling their chances for a match. However, in Mark's case because his blood type was O, we were limited even more. Blood family members are most likely to result in a successful transplant so they like to look at family first. Mark had seven siblings who all got tested to see if they had the same blood type as Mark. His mother also was tested (his father had passed away).

Three brothers had the same blood type as Mark. His other four siblings and mother had type B blood. Many times during the transplant process I asked God why Mark couldn't have type B instead of one of his other siblings. Then any of the siblings could have donated. It seemed cruel that Mark had a 50/50 chance of making this much easier, and he was dealt the hard hand....again.

Because of the high cost, the Transplant Center would only test one possible donor at a time. Donors have to go through a lot of testing before they can be considered for a transplant to make sure their body can donate a kidney safely and can handle the stress of a major surgery.

Mark's brother, Buddy, was the first to undergo the testing. He went through all the testing, and we set a transplant date of November 27, 2001. Mark underwent the testing that he had to have done again due to the heart surgery. Finally, he was finished and had passed all the testing. He was approved for the transplant. It looked like it was finally going to happen!

Mark and Buddy had some final testing the day before the scheduled transplant. This took all day for both of them. At the end of a very long day, while Mark was in dialysis (for what we hoped was the last time), Buddy was recovering from an invasive procedure to determine which kidney could be used. And then we got devastating news.

The kidney has vessels that supply blood to it. Normally a kidney has one to two vessels. Rarely will a kidney have more. One of Buddy's kidneys had four vessels while the other kidney had two but also had a possible cyst. The transplant team prefers to have one vessel to work with as there is a better chance for the kidney to work in the recipient. They will perform a kidney transplant with two vessels, but won't if a kidney has more than two. Unfortunately, because one of Buddy's kidney had four vessels and the other kidney had the possible cyst, Buddy was ruled out as a potential donor. The night before the transplant, everything fell through.

It was crushing news, again. We were so close. It was like being on a sinking ship. Every time we thought the shore was getting closer, another storm pushed us further away from the safety of the shore.

The doctor told us (Buddy, Mark's sister, and me) the news while Mark was receiving dialysis. I insisted that I tell this heart-wrenching news to Mark rather than the doctors. I wanted Mark to hear it from me. He was alone while he was receiving dialysis, and I didn't want him to hear it without support by his side. Telling him was the hardest thing I've had to do. When I told him, he tried to hide it, but I could tell he was crushed. His face fell. I knew he was disappointed. But then he looked up and said, "We need to make sure Buddy is okay." He was concerned about the possible cyst on his kidney and what that could mean for his brother.

Mark impressed me that day. He had a chance to finally feel better after years of feeling miserable, but he was focused on Buddy and making sure he was okay. He was truly a selfless man in that moment. He could have been bitter, angry, and depressed. Nobody would have blamed him. But he chose to be loving and giving. Mark never focused on himself. He always worried about other people and being there for others. That special quality in him inspired me to do the same. I knew I would do everything I could to protect and focus on him like he did for others.

Not long after Buddy was disqualified as a donor his second brother, Paul, was tested. He didn't want us to hear the devastating news the day before the transplant like with Buddy, so he adamantly demanded all testing to happen before the transplant. We were glad he insisted on it. In a rare turn of events, Paul's kidneys each had three vessels. He was ruled out as a donor.

I could tell Mark was losing hope. He put up a brave face when Paul told us the devastating news. Paul had wanted the news to come from him and not from the Transplant Center in hopes it would be easier to hear it from him. Mark thanked him for telling us even though Paul said it was one of the hardest things he ever had to do.

After Paul told us the news and left our house, Mark told me he was okay, but I knew he wasn't. For days, he had a hard time getting out of bed. The fatigue from dialysis already made it so he slept most of the time, but after hearing Paul had been ruled out as a donor, he was sleeping even more. He was depressed, and I couldn't blame him. I was depressed too, but I tried hard to be strong for him. Some days, though, I found a corner and cried alone. I just couldn't be strong all the time.

We were down to his last eligible brother and truthfully Mark's last hope for a chance of a successful transplant. His brother, Scott, also demanded all the testing be done ahead of time and at this point the Transplant Center also agreed without question. Scott's first kidney had two vessels and the other one had three.

Normally they would continue testing donors to find one with one vessel. But at this point, the doctors knew the options were limited. They knew Mark's chances of a successful transplant would be better with a kidney with only one vessel, but his health was failing. They thought a transplant was his best hope and it had to be done soon. Dialysis was already taking a major toll on Mark's body and his heart. Dialysis is life-saving and necessary, but it is hard on the body. We had been told that the majority of patients who pass away on dialysis die from heart attacks and heart failure rather than kidney failure because dialysis makes the heart work much harder.

It looked promising that the transplant would be happening and we breathed another sigh of relief. Before the kidney transplant could happen, Mark had to undergo routine labs and tests again as it had been awhile since they had been done with the two failed donors.

Urgh. More testing.

He had several vials of blood drawn and everything was looking pretty good on the blood work. So far, so good!

Then he underwent an echocardiogram, which is an ultrasound of the heart. We were shocked to discover between November 2001 and January 2002, Mark had had a silent heart attack, and now had severe heart damage. His heart was only pumping at 15 percent which was very low. A healthy person would normally have a heart pumping at about 70 percent. There was no way to determine when this silent heart attack had occurred. Mark couldn't remember having any symptoms during that time. But there was evidence that he had had a heart attack and suddenly a kidney transplant became a very high risk, again.

I was working at St. Croix Regional Medical Center as a medical transcriptionist when I got the phone call. I will never forget that moment. The phone often rang at my desk so hearing the phone ring wasn't unusual. But I had no idea that when I picked up the phone this time our lives would take another dramatic turn.

"We strongly recommend Mark gets evaluated for a heart transplant before going ahead with the kidney transplant," our transplant coordinator told me.

Time froze. My heart dropped. I started shaking and almost dropped the phone. I thought I heard wrong. This couldn't be happening.

"What?"

"I'm so sorry Tammy. I've been dreading making this call. His heart function is so low, and his heart is so weak. We think the kidney transplant might be too hard on the heart. We think this is the best. I'm really very sorry."

I could hardly talk. This was impossible to process. I felt like I was living a nightmare. We already had two brothers denied as donors and the third, and last eligible, brother barely approved. Now that we finally had a transplant surgery date, we were faced with this?

I couldn't hold back the tears. I cut off the conversation as quickly as I could and hung up the phone. I sat at my desk bawling until I could get my composure. I couldn't stay at work. I knew I wouldn't be able to concentrate. My world was crashing. It took all the strength I had to find my boss and tell her what I had found out. She was shocked and didn't know what to say. She gave me a hug and said, "Go. Just go. We'll take care of everything here." I'm grateful I had the support of my co-workers and a supportive and caring work environment.

Telling Mark was hard. Normally he's a positive person but this news cut deep. After I told him, he looked defeated. I told him he couldn't give up. He responded with, "Yes, I can."

My stomach dropped hearing him say those words. I felt sick. He was normally strong and positive. If he was giving up, what did it mean? We always leaned on each other. I started panicking as I felt the strength leaving my body. I needed him to be strong in order for me to be strong. I didn't blame him though. I wanted to give up, and I wasn't in his shoes.

How much heartache could one person go through?

After much discussion with the transplant team and the cardiovascular team they decided to proceed with the transplant even though it was a "high risk". A cardiologist needed to be there during the surgery. We were told there was a 50/50 chance of death. If he survived the kidney transplant, they wanted him to be evaluated for a heart transplant after he recovered. At that point, they believed having a new kidney would put less stress on his weak heart, so they agreed to do the kidney transplant first. It seemed like there was no end in sight. We focused on taking one step at a time. First, we were going to focus on the kidney transplant.

On March 21, 2002, Mark received a kidney from his brother, Scott. It wasn't an easy surgery. It lasted a couple hours longer than they said it would. There were complications. Mark had a heart attack during the transplant surgery. Somehow, despite all the complications, Mark survived. It was, in no doubt, because God had plans for Mark. He worked through the medical team, and the surgery was ultimately successful.

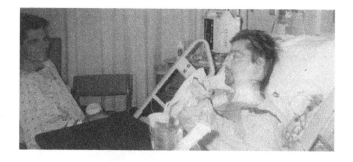

Mark sees Scott (his donor) for the first time after the surgery

Mark's recovery wasn't easy. We figured it would take longer for him to get his strength back, so we weren't surprised. Mark always seemed to do things on his own time.

It was a blessing for me to watch Mark amaze the doctors continuously. Not just in regard to the success of his kidney transplant, but for years afterward. The doctors told us we would be "very fortunate" if his kidney lasted ten years (his kidney lasted the rest of his life, about 17-1/2 years!). We were told Mark had a 75 percent chance of having some sort of rejection episode. During the 17-1/2 years, he never had one. "Medical miracles," they said. It truly was a miracle.

The transplant brought Scott and Mark much closer. I loved watching the bond they shared. The first time they saw each other was about a month after the transplant when my sister-in-law, Carole, took Mark to see Scott. Scott had struggled with some issues after the transplant and it was taking longer for him to recover. Mark wanted to see him and make sure he was okay. Carole told me she would never forget that feeling when they saw each other for the first time after the transplant. Mark's eyes lit up seeing his brother. Scott had a look of surprise and relief as he saw Mark walking towards him. Mark looked much better to Scott than he did before the transplant. It was a magical moment, and she knew they would have a special bond for life.

Throughout the years, they were always saying "I love you," hugging, and calling on a regular basis. It was a special relationship that few could understand and a bond no one else could ever take away.

I am so grateful to donors, living and deceased, as they give a gift no one could ever imagine. I want to give a kidney to someone. God will let me know when the time is right. I've had a couple chances, but God has closed the doors. One day, though, I hope the door will open. God gave us two kidneys, one to keep and one to share. I plan to share mine with someone so they will have their own story to share.

Now if this was the end of the amazing miracles we have experienced, we would consider us blessed and honored to be recipients of God's grace. But that isn't the end of the medical miracles of Mark.

———————— ✦✦✦✦✦✦ ————————

A couple years after the kidney transplant, in 2004, things started settling down. Mark decided to get evaluated for a potential heart transplant. I knew the kidney transplant was very hard on him, and I didn't want him to feel like he had to go through anything like that again so I left the decision completely up to him. After a couple years of success with the kidney, he wanted to do anything to extend his life, even if it meant another transplant surgery. He said life was too good not to do everything possible to be healthy. The dream of purchasing our own home and possibly starting a family were important to us. I was terrified and anxious. I also felt honored and humbled that Mark would be willing to go through another transplant in hopes of a better and healthier future with me.

We knew this was going to be another hard journey. We were basically starting over with all the testing we had previously done. We spent one whole day at the Transplant Center to get all the testing and meetings they wanted done. Going through tests after tests, going through the whole process step-by-step, so many steps people don't even realize. It is grueling.

We met with a heart transplant support group which was a requirement. Going to a transplant support group is quite an eye-opener. We were surrounded by at least twenty people who had had a heart transplant or were waiting for one. A few people had been in the hospital for months waiting for a heart. These people wouldn't be able to leave until they received a heart because they were dependent on machines to live. There is a huge need for organs, a much bigger need than most people realize.

As we were moving through the evaluations, we weren't told the results of the tests as we went along. We just showed up where and when they wanted us to. There was one rather invasive test where they made an incision near his heart and went in to examine the heart functionality. It was the last test of the day. It took a couple hours, and I had to wait in the waiting room. I was worried what they were going to find, and it was a long couple hours.

When the doctor came out, he had a smile on his face, "Well, Tammy, we're done. Everything went well, and his heart looks pretty good!"

I was shocked and confused. Honestly, that wasn't the news I was expecting, "Are you sure?"

The doctor kinda laughed and said, "Yes. It's really not that bad, and I certainly don't think he needs a heart transplant, at least not yet."

I was dumbfounded. He did not need a heart transplant. His heart wasn't bad enough for a heart transplant! His heart function had actually increased. A normal ejection fraction is 60-70 percent. Right before the kidney transplant, it had gone down to 15 percent. It typically never gets better. At the time of these tests, his function had actually gone up to 25 percent. There was no medical explanation for it. Years later, his heart function continued improving and eventually got as high as 40 percent. It was truly shocking as that just doesn't happen. It's a miracle which I love sharing.

I tell that story because we believe God performed a miracle. He improved Mark's heart when every doctor told us he wouldn't survive, that he needed a transplant, and his heart would not improve. God proved them wrong and again Mark beat the odds.

———————— ⁘⬥⬥⬥⬥⁘ ————————

In 2016, we experienced yet another miracle. Again, God intervened to prove doctors' predictions wrong. That summer, his kidney numbers on his lab work started creeping up a little bit. This meant the kidney wasn't working as well as it should be. By fall, the numbers increased even more. Even more terrifying was that Mark was having more and more protein in his urine, a definite sign of kidney failure.

We were told that the most likely cause was chronic rejection. Because his kidney was almost fifteen years post transplant and complicated by Mark's diabetes, it was thought that the kidney was wearing out. It was devastating for Mark. Even knowing that he was still a few years away from needing dialysis if chronic rejection was the case, he had a hard time feeling positive. Dialysis had been hard on him. He had told me he never wanted to go through it again.

The doctor recommended Mark have a kidney biopsy to determine the exact cause for his kidney numbers and protein in the urine to be increasing. We were hesitant at first. We knew if it was chronic rejection, there was nothing they could do. In our minds, we didn't want to go through an invasive procedure only to be given bad news. However, that tiny bit of hope that it wasn't chronic rejection convinced us to go ahead with the biopsy.

Just a couple days before the procedure, I got a call from Mark's nephrologist (kidney doctor). He said the latest tests, taken a few days prior, showed there was more protein in the urine and his kidney numbers were even higher.

"I just wanted to prepare you for the fact that we will most likely see some chronic rejection in the biopsy. I know it's disappointing but that doesn't mean he'll lose the kidney right away."

I couldn't tell Mark. I knew that would destroy him. We never kept secrets from each other. I felt guilty not telling him, but I wanted him to have some hope. I held onto that small hope and miracle that they wouldn't find rejection. I never told Mark about that phone call.

Mark had the biopsy done. We waited three long days before our transplant coordinator called with the results.

"Well, Tammy, I have good news! There is no rejection!"

I thought I heard her wrong, "Um, really? Are you sure?"

She laughed a little and said, "Yep, I'm sure. I've got the report right here. I'll read it to you."

She went ahead and read the report word for word. There were many medical terms but also very thorough examination and tested different antibodies for rejection. I heard our coordinator tell me several times as she was reading the report of the antibodies, "No rejection", "No rejection."

I had tears of joy listening to her read the report! I couldn't help but smile as I thanked her for giving us the wonderful and hopeful news. It was music to my ears. Another miracle of many that Mark has been given. Another example of Mark beating the odds.

I firmly believe that medical practice is necessary. Without it, Mark wouldn't have lived past four years of age. He lived a longer and better quality of life due to the field of medicine. I believe God gives the knowledge and expertise needed to the medical professionals to do the work they need to. For that I am so grateful.

I also believe in the power of God and with God, anything is possible. Mark is proof. He truly was a walking miracle, not just once but time and time again.

CHAPTER 4

INFERTILITY—IUIs (INTRAUTERINE INSEMINATIONS)

As I mentioned before, I always wanted kids. I had it all planned out. Mark laughed when I told him I had planned to marry a farmer. Mark was much more a city boy than a country boy. He was definitely not a farmer.

When Mark and I got married in 2001, we didn't plan on having kids. To be honest, I thought with Mark's health, he wouldn't live long enough. I anticipated we would be blessed to be married five years before he passed away. Loving Mark and taking care of him was my first priority, not having kids. I wanted to cherish the time I had with Mark while I could. I had always wanted to be a mom, but when I married Mark, I didn't think it would be possible. Although I was disappointed and sad, I figured being Mark's wife and taking care of him was the road God had chosen for me.

But I was wrong, God chose differently for us.

In 2002, our nephew, Tyler, was born. He was the first baby in our family, and we instantly fell in love with him. The longing to have a baby of our own increased for both of us. We decided we wanted to try to have a baby. Making that decision was hard for us.

Were we doing the right thing? Were we being selfish bringing a child into the world with Mark having so many health issues? Was it fair to the child to deal with so much? What would people think? These were questions we were constantly battling with.

On the other hand, I really wanted a part of Mark to live on, especially if he were to pass away. My dream was to have a girl who looked just like her daddy. I wanted to be a mom so badly and my desire kept getting stronger. Mark's desire for a daughter matched mine. Initially with his age and health issues, he wasn't too interested in "starting over". He already had two boys from his previous marriage. He also saw how important it was to me to have a baby. He desperately wanted to make me happy. With time and with God's touch on Mark's heart, his desire for a baby increased.

So we put our faith in God and not on what others thought. After all, no child's life is perfect. All children have their own struggles in different ways. Our child may have to deal with some hard times with a parent being chronically ill, but there were other struggles she or he wouldn't have to deal with that other kids would.

Never in a million years did we think we would have trouble conceiving—never. My mom had no problems at all (she even had fraternal twins). My sister would just "look" at her husband and get pregnant. Mark had his two boys. We felt the odds were good for having a baby pretty easily.

But God had a different plan for us.

At first when we started trying, we were nervous but excited and hopeful! We figured it wouldn't take long at all before we were announcing to our family and friends that I was pregnant.

Month after month went by. We were living in two-week intervals. Anxiously awaiting the perfect time and then two weeks later anxiously awaiting to see if we were pregnant.

After months of not becoming pregnant, the excitement of trying to have a baby turned into frustration, sadness, and helplessness. Although we always felt some hope, it was getting harder and harder to remain positive. When we first started our journey, we had decided that if having a baby didn't happen the "natural" way, we weren't going to talk to doctors. We thought if God wanted us to have a baby, we would have one the way we were intended. We didn't want to seek a doctor's help.

You know where this is going, don't you?

Yes, God changed our hearts.

One thing we learned going through the kidney transplant was that without medical intervention, Mark wouldn't be here. Our pastor told us that with God and medical intervention, anything is possible. Turning to medical intervention doesn't mean we don't trust God. In fact, we wholeheartedly believed God works through medicine to help people heal.

After a few years of not being able to get pregnant and after much prayer, we decided to seek doctor's assistance. It wasn't easy to seek advice from medical doctors on such an intimate subject, especially for Mark. He could easily talk about motorcycles for hours but talking about my feminine cycles made him seize up like an engine without oil.

With a doctor's help, we went through a procedure called intrauterine insemination where the sperm was placed into my uterus to help with fertilization. My doctors really got to know me. I felt like I had no privacy at all. We were in constant contact talking about my body and when we thought I was ovulating. We had to try to pinpoint the best time for the procedure to take place for our best chances of pregnancy. We were living our lives in two-week intervals again, only this time doctors were living it with us. There was a constant circle of emotions from hope to devastation and back again.

We went through a total of twelve intrauterine inseminations. Normally, doctors don't recommend doing that many. We were told that with every unsuccessful insemination, your chance of success decreases. In the first three cycles, your chance of success is about twenty percent. If you do six cycles, your chances are about six percent. After six cycles, we were told we needed to seriously consider the next step. The next step was in vitro fertilization, also called IVF.

This was a treatment that we had mixed moral feelings. It was for these reasons, that we continued to do as many inseminations as we did. But when the twelfth insemination wasn't successful, I knew in my heart this wasn't the direction to go anymore. We needed to move in a different direction.

I don't regret doing the twelve inseminations. With each insemination, I learned something new or went through something that changed my life or taught me important lessons. For that I am incredibly grateful. We took a wonderful trip to Hawaii after the twelfth insemination as a way to take a break, physically and mentally. Our doctor actually "ordered" us to go. I remember booking the airline tickets and hotel and thinking, "Oh great. That could have been another insemination and that could have been the one that worked!" I was actually annoyed at our doctor for "making" us go to Hawaii when we could have used that money more wisely. Looking back I realize just how obsessed I was with inseminations. I was annoyed we were using money to go to Hawaii. For normal people spending money to go to Hawaii is a dream come true.

We had always wanted to go to Hawaii. I'm truly glad we went. After going through so much devastation, we deserved a little happiness. It was a wonderful experience and it was one we would cherish. I know without going through the devastation, we probably wouldn't have justified the trip. We deserved it, and it was such a needed vacation. It refreshed us.

When we returned home, it was time to make a decision about IVF. It wasn't going to be an easy one.

CHAPTER 5

INFERTILITY--IVF (IN VITRO FERTILIZATION)

It was now summer of 2009, and the sixth year of struggling to conceive. Going through IVF was something we wanted to do only if we felt comfortable with the idea and it was God driven. We know some people are completely against it, and we respect their moral opinions and beliefs. Ultimately, we wanted to do what was right for us and what God was leading us to do. We wanted to follow His direction, not ours, or other peoples' beliefs.

During an IVF cycle, the goal is to try and retrieve as many eggs from the woman's body as possible and of good quality. Then, each egg (hopefully) fertilizes when it comes in contact with sperm outside of the womb. In our belief, when a sperm and egg come together, there is always a possibility of a life. Life begins at fertilization. We knew if there was fertilization, called an embryo, it would be watched carefully for a few days. If it wasn't continuing to grow, it would be discarded. If it continued to grow, the embryo could be transferred into a woman's body to hopefully continue to grow to full-term. Extra viable embryos can be frozen for future use.

The process bothered us when we first looked into it. In our minds, we would be creating multiple babies to get the "best" ones. An embryo is a baby and we couldn't imagine deciding which were "good" and "bad". The thought of our child being "discarded" really bothered us. It felt like we would be throwing our children away. The thought that some embryos could be determined to be "better" than others also bothered us. The idea of freezing embryos bothered us too! Our babies would be frozen! There were a lot of things that seemed to bother us about the whole process. Also, for example, if they transferred three embryos into my body and if we were blessed that one did stick but two did not, that would mean two of our children died in our minds.

There were so many emotional conflicts, and we just didn't know how to handle it. There were many factors and concerns, and we were conflicted about what to do. Were we doing the right thing by going forward?

Besides the moral conflict, the expense of IVF also weighed heavily on our minds. IVF is expensive. It would not be covered by our health insurance and would cost about $10,000.

We talked about our confusing feelings with other couples who had gone through the process and also talked with various pastors. We realized that if we decided to go through IVF, every single embryo that was created would be a child in our minds. If embryos weren't growing and were discarded or didn't implant, it would be okay to mourn the babies. It would be a loss of life. We knew those children were created in love with the desire for them to have a precious life with us. They would not be a casual loss. Each one was given a name. Each one was cherished. Each one was hoped for. Each one was mourned. Each one taught us the preciousness of life. We knew a lost child could never be replaced, but its existence and loss could make our bond stronger and our future more meaningful.

Understandably, while grief of embryo loss may not be as profound as other child losses, it still was painful and tremendously sad. We consoled ourselves by thinking no one would question grief if we conceived a baby naturally and it didn't make it to full-term, was stillborn, died as an infant, or if the baby grew into a child or teen but was accidentally killed. In those cases, grief would also be felt by others because the child was loved and cherished. Loving someone for any length of time leads to grief if her or his life ends. Just because others didn't know embryo deaths didn't make them less deserving of love or grief.

We also came to realize that God created us and gave us technology. Sometimes technology is a blessing. As long as we err on the side of compassion and love, leaving our hearts and minds open to all the possibilities God offers, God blesses our efforts.

We were grateful to have others to talk to who would be honest with us and wouldn't judge our feelings and decisions. After much discussion, thought, and prayer, we decided to take a leap of faith and try IVF.

It was a huge step and a big decision. Not only was it expensive, it would involve giving myself shots of hormones every day. We would have to travel about an hour one way to the doctor's office almost every day. I would have a lot of blood work done and undergo a procedure that would require me to be put under anesthesia. Oh, and somehow managing to fit this into my full-time work schedule.

It was not easy to go through it. It was hard to give myself shots. I was bloated and tired all the time. Making many trips to the doctor's office was time consuming and exhausting. But we knew this was our best chance to have a baby.

The night before we went in for the egg retrieval, Mark had to give me a shot of HCG, also known as the "pregnancy hormone". When injected, HCG causes a woman to ovulate about thirty-six hours later. Imagine the biggest needle you've ever seen in your life. Now imagine a needle three times that big. That needle was stuck into my body. Okay, I may be exaggerating but it was ONE. BIG. NEEDLE. I remember when we were going through the shot training class and the nurse showed us the needle. Both Mark's and my eyes popped out of our heads. "That's one BIG needle!" I said. The nurse, being very supportive (big use of sarcasm there) said, "Actually this isn't that big. The one you have to use is actually much bigger. We just use this for training."

Thanks for the encouragement.

I was nervous at the egg retrieval procedure and Mark could tell. He was sweet and would get me laughing and relaxed. That helped. At one point when they had me change into my gown, Mark said, "You know, we could switch places. I don't think they would suspect a thing." He could always make me laugh.

The most special part was when I first woke up from the anesthesia and I saw Mark standing right next to me with a smile on his face. He asked me if I had heard how many eggs were retrieved and I told him I hadn't. He was so proud to tell me they retrieved twelve eggs. It was special to hear it from Mark and not a nurse or doctor. Not that they aren't good people, but to hear it from Mark was just better. I don't remember much, but Mark said I was pretty out of it and kept repeating myself. He told me I kept saying over and over, "Can you believe it? We're going to be parents!" at least a dozen times. Obviously, I was pretty excited.

I remember someone saying that after the retrieval, they felt a sense of loss when the eggs were retrieved. I could understand what they meant. It was a little sad for me to realize that those twelve eggs that we had seen on ultrasounds for the last couple weeks were no longer in me. We had watched them grow right there on the screen. Granted, I also knew it was a good thing and I was excited, but there was still a sense of loss and a little sadness. I wasn't expecting to feel that way over eggs.

The clinic promised to call us the next day to tell us how the embryos were growing. I thought about our twelve embryos constantly. Like a protective mother, I just wanted to be there and watch them. I wanted to make sure they were okay and being treated right. I couldn't wait for the next day to hear how they were doing.

We had what one nurse called a "perfect cycle". I was told that compared to the women who were in the same cycle as me at that clinic, it looked like I would have the best outcome based on the number of eggs retrieved and labs that were completed. That was encouraging news to us. I was pretty optimistic that we were going to get awesome news.

The nurse called the next day. We were driving on the road just outside of town with cars behind us and also traveling towards us in the other lane. When I saw the call come in, I pulled over to the side of the road so I could focus on what the nurse had to say.

"This is it, Mark!" I excitedly said. This was the call we had been anxiously waiting for all morning. We were going to be scheduling the embryo transfer based on how well the embryos were growing. I was optimistic about the news we were about to hear. I couldn't have been prepared for what she said.

Of the twelve embryos, only four fertilized, and none of them had started to divide or grow, which they should have by that time. There would be no transfer. No pregnancy. Our babies were gone. It was over.

We were shocked and devastated.

When we got the news, we were on our way to a toy show where we going to be selling toys to earn some money for the IVF cycle. I was crying hard, and Mark and I held each other for the longest time. I could hear cars whizzing by as I sobbed in Mark's arms. I felt angry and kept asking "Why?". I was devastated as I watched other cars being able to "travel forward" past us while our world was crashing around us and in a sense we were at a standstill. How dare they continue on with their lives like nothing had happened? Did they know they were driving by people whose lives were just turned upside down? Our parents graciously took our toys and went to the show for us. It was a cruel irony that we had to "turn around" because our plans, once again, were dashed. I started our car, eyes red and swollen from crying so hard. It took strength to turn the blinker on and wait for a space between cars to drive back into traffic. Turning around and going back home was incredibly difficult.

The doctor called us a few hours later. The first thing the doctor said when he talked to us on the phone was, "This is a disaster." Of course, that wasn't what I needed to hear and the tears just flowed. He said what happened was very uncommon, although he had seen it before. I was the first case that year and he sees a lot of patients. This was in October so the fact that I was the first that year said a lot as to how uncommon it was. Our doctor was very compassionate. He was comforting to me even though it hurt so very badly.

I wrote this letter shortly after that horrible day.

To our babies,

The day we started our IVF, I looked forward to knowing you were inside my tummy and hoping and praying that in nine months you would be born healthy and happy.

I'm sad it didn't turn out the way we had hoped, but I'm happy you guys are in Heaven and safely sitting on Jesus' lap.

I don't regret doing the IVF at all. Your daddy and I loved going to the ultrasounds and watching those eggs grow. We knew we were watching our babies grow. Every shot, bruise, and all the side effects were worth being able to see you guys.

I regret that I didn't get more pictures at the ultrasounds. If I would have known those were the only pictures I would have of you guys, I would have had them print out as many as they could every time we went in.

I also regret that I was never able to have that feeling of knowing you guys were in my tummy. I never had the feeling of "being pregnant until proven otherwise". I really wish I could have had that chance, and I'm sad that I wasn't able to. In some ways I feel like I failed you as your mommy because I wasn't able to get to that final step where you would know you were so loved and where you could feel the warmth of love from my tummy and heart.

I wish I could have done more. I feel like a bad mommy because I wasn't there to protect you. I feel like I should have driven down to the lab on Saturday when there was still a little hope. As your mommy, I feel I should have been there. I know there was nothing I could do, but as your mommy, I wanted to protect you. I'm sorry I couldn't do more. I hope you know how many people were praying for you guys. We have many friends and family who love us. There was much love around you guys that day.

Please know that even though we only had you guys in our lives for a few days, for those few days, we had much hope and love. We couldn't stop thinking about you guys. We wouldn't give that up for anything.

I know one day we'll see each other again. I know Jesus is holding you tight in His arms until Daddy and I see you. I know you guys are in the best hands you can be, but I'm jealous that Jesus gets to hold you before I do.

I know Jesus has a plan, and I know you guys know that, too. Jesus has probably already shared it with you. I know you don't understand why I'm sad when Jesus has such great plans for me. I know it's hard to understand. As much as I know it'll all work out for the best, I miss you guys. I really wish I could hold you-just once.

I'd do this all over again if we had another chance. I'd do it in a heartbeat, and I'd do as many shots as I needed to. I would just make sure I would get more pictures at the ultrasounds. I would also ask more questions to the nurse during it so I could see you guys longer--just in case those were the only times we would get to know you.

There isn't a day your daddy and I don't think about you guys. Our hearts ache, and we have never felt this kind of pain. We know you don't want us to be sad. It's hard to understand why we are sad when you guys are so happy. We are just hurting knowing we can't see or feel you every day. I guess you can say you have a selfish mommy and daddy.

Please watch over us, our dear angels. Show us the way to go next. Please give us the strength to be able to carry on. We miss you and love you more than you can ever know. We can't wait to see you guys and hold you in our arms.

With all my love forever,
Mommy

Our doctor wanted to try to find out answers about what happened. There were several couples who had embryos in that exact same lab as us. The first step was to make sure the other embryos were okay to rule out an equipment malfunction. The other embryos were growing just as they should. That ruled out an equipment malfunction.

The next step was to run additional blood work to see if there was anything that would explain what happened. After performing some tests, they found I have a rare genetic disorder. My eggs could fertilize, but once fertilized, they would just stop growing. Our doctor had been working in the infertility field for over thirty years, and he had only heard of this happening to two other women. This particular disorder was so rare (and the testing was very expensive), so it was only done in this type of situation. That was why it took so long to notice. All those IUIs, all those years of trying and testing, it was never going to happen. No matter what we tried or did. I would never be able to have a baby with my eggs.

I realize that if we had known about the genetic disorder from the beginning, it would have saved a lot of money and heartache. However, looking back I don't regret any of the time, money, or heartache that we went through. While it certainly wasn't easy, I believe it made us stronger as a couple and stronger in our faith. The lessons in life we learned along the way were priceless to us.

However, this news was devastating beyond measure to me. I felt like a failure. Failure as a woman, failure to my husband, failure to my friends and family. I couldn't understand how this was happening. I honestly didn't think Mark would want to be married to me anymore. I felt like damaged goods. Women were supposed to create babies. They were supposed to get pregnant. I couldn't do that, and it was hard to accept.

Of course Mark wanted to still be married to me and neither one of us felt like giving up. Our hearts desire was to have a baby. As long as the desire was still there, we felt God was leading our hearts to keep trying, just to go in a different direction.

After the news about my genetic disorder, we had a long talk with our doctor. We could try what they call an embryo transfer using donated or adopted embryos. These would be embryos that were created during another couple's IVF cycle. If the couple has a successful IVF cycle, they may end up with extra embryos that they choose to freeze rather than discard or donate to science. The couple can make decisions on what they would like to do with their extra embryos. Sometimes if a couple has a successful pregnancy and prefers not to pursue another pregnancy, they choose to donate the embryos to another couple in situations like ours. It is similar to an adoption of a baby or a child.

I still had a strong desire to be pregnant. My desire to be pregnant was almost as strong as the desire to be a mother and have a baby in my arms. To some, that may not make sense. But to me, feeling my baby inside of me was something I desperately wanted. I wanted to feel the morning sickness. I wanted to feel the baby's kicks and hiccups. I wanted that feeling of being uncomfortable. I wanted to go through labor. I desperately wanted to experience a pregnancy. I wanted to see that positive pregnancy test and be able to tell people, "I'm pregnant!"

My heart really wasn't ready to give up that dream. I just couldn't do it.

So we decided to take the next step and look into donated embryos.

CHAPTER 6

INFERTILITY--DONATED EMBRYOS/FETS (FROZEN EMBRYO TRANSFERS)

Again, we were faced with a difficult decision. Like IVF, we didn't take this lightly. There were many things to think about. In a typical frozen embryo transfer using donated embryos, which is what we would be doing, three embryos are taken out to thaw. The hope is that two will survive the thaw and able to be transferred into the uterus with at least one "sticking" inside the woman's uterus. From the medical field's point of view, this was the best chance to become pregnant. When we thought about this, we felt like we were losing two babies to have one.

Also, we had to think of the possibility if all three survived the thaw? Would we transfer all three? What if all three stuck? Then there would be the possibility of triplets or even more. In such cases, we would need to consider an embryo reduction. During this procedure, they would terminate one baby in order to have a less risky pregnancy for the other two babies. We didn't think that was morally right.

Other scenarios needed to be considered as well. If we adopted a set of four embryos, and we used three embryos for one cycle, what would we do with the last embryo? Would we keep it frozen, knowing chances were so low for a successful transfer with only one embryo?

There was so much to think about. There were different circumstances and situations that could happen. We had to think of all the possible outcomes. For us, it was a complicated moral decision more than anything. While we understood the science part of an embryo transfer and how they based success on statistics, we believed life began at conception and every embryo was a baby. It was hard to think of embryos as anything but human life and yet we wanted to do what was best to have a successful transfer. It was hard to find a common ground.

We thought about it. We talked about it together and with others. We prayed about it, a lot. We didn't want to compromise our morals to have a successful transfer, even if that meant our odds for success weren't as good.

We came to realize was that nothing is ever guaranteed. Just like during the IVF process, a baby would be created. A baby would be loved. A baby would be mourned. A lost child could never be replaced, but its existence and loss could make our bond stronger and future more meaningful. We also felt certain this is the way God sees it too. Life starts at conception and each embryo was a life. Would He mourn a loss of life if an embryo didn't make it through a transfer? Of course. He mourns at any loss of life.

We decided to go ahead with a frozen embryo transfer after much thought and prayer. We wouldn't compromise our moral beliefs. We would not thaw more than two at a time. We would not reduce multiple transferred embryos. We would love and pray for each embryo, whether they made it two days, twenty years, or more. With that in mind, we set our hearts on proceeding with a frozen embryo transfer. Adopting embryos with the hopes of my dream of being pregnant was going to become a reality. We were excited to start the process!

It wasn't long after we made the decision to adopt embryos that a friend contacted me in November 2009. She was pregnant with twins after going through an IVF cycle. She was due to deliver in January 2010. They had a set of three frozen embryos from their IVF cycle. If she completed a successful pregnancy with a healthy delivery, she knew they would be adopting out the embryos. She wondered if we would be interested in adopting them.

We were ecstatic! Of course we wanted to adopt them!

She had two months left in her pregnancy. It was the longest two months ever. We were all thrilled when she gave birth to two healthy babies and we could proceed with the embryo adoption.

We had to legally adopt the three embryos. Once the legal paperwork was completed, we started getting ready for the frozen transfer. The embryos were stored in Michigan. It would be better for the embryos if they stayed where they were stored rather than ship them to Minnesota where our clinic was located at. So we decided to use the clinic in Michigan rather than our clinic. This was not going to be easy. It's hard enough trying to coordinate a transfer when you live close to the clinic, but trying to time a transfer with doctors out of state was very difficult. I still had to take shots and get blood work done. That could be done at my local clinic, but the doctors in Michigan would make all medical decisions because they were the ones ultimately performing the transfer. Our clinic would do the lab draws and then fax the results over to the clinic in Michigan. The doctor there would make decisions and coordinate my medication dosages and dates of transfer.

It was a lot to deal with, but we were finally given permission to have the transfer done. We booked a flight to Michigan. We met with the doctor and made a plan for the transfer the next day. We had three embryos available. They were all considered excellent embryos based on how they had grown. Embryos are graded based on "poor" to "excellent". In our minds, it was hard to consider any embryos better than others morally, but medically they used this system to measure their success rates. Based on the fact that we had three "excellent" embryos, they said our chances for success were very good.

The doctor stated they were only comfortable transferring two embryos. They suggested thawing three embryos with the hope of having at least two survive the thaw. If all three survived, they would transfer the two best ones and discard the third. While we knew this would make for the best success rate, it was hard to think like that. We explained to the doctor that we only wanted two embryos thawed. We didn't want three thawed with the hope that two would survive. We didn't want the mindset of hoping one embryo died. We agreed that if two were thawed out and one didn't make it, then the last one would be thawed. We didn't want any "discarded" if at all possible.

While I was getting prepped for the transfer, the embryos were thawed out. Just before they took me back to the transfer room to have the embryos transferred into my uterus, the doctor came into the preoperative room with a picture of two beautiful embryos.

"Do you want to see the first picture of your babies?"

I'll never forget that moment when I saw the picture of the embryos. I was so happy.

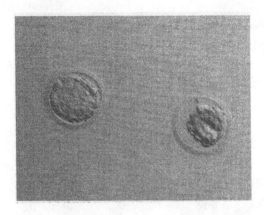

The first picture of our babies our doctor handed to us

But then he said something that took my breath away.

"We had to thaw all three. One of the embryos didn't make it."

Then the doctor started explaining the procedure. I didn't hear much of it to be honest. When he said one of the embryos didn't make it, my first thought was *My baby died.* I was mourning, and I couldn't stop thinking about my sweet baby who didn't make it. It was hard to put aside my grief, but I also knew I had to focus on the transfer. I was about to have two babies inserted into me! I was going to be pregnant with twins!

In order to place the embryos in the best position, the doctor had a camera to help guide them. It was all shown on a big screen that we were able to watch. As Mark held my hand, we watched as the doctor placed the embryos into my uterus. It was a feeling of awe and wonder that I would never forget.

I was required to have strict bed rest for forty-eight hours following the transfer. We stayed in a hotel room for two full days. I was so careful not to do anything that would disrupt my babies.

When I was finally off bed rest, we made plans to meet my friend who had donated her embryos to us. Meeting her and her beautiful twin girls was the most amazing and emotional experience ever. I'll never forget that first hug, wrapping my arms around her, and sobbing. I knew she would always be special to me. She gave me a gift for which I could never thank her enough. She gave me the opportunity to be a mom and be pregnant, which was a dream for me. We went out to eat at Panera Bread, loved up on her babies, talked, and laughed together.

Then we said goodbye. Saying goodbye was tough. I felt I was saying goodbye to a precious member of the family, and in a sense, I was. I knew she would always be considered a special part of our family.

We flew back to Wisconsin and went through the dreaded two-week wait yet again. Two weeks after the transfer, I was scheduled for a beta test. A beta test is a blood test to determine if you are pregnant, and if the transfer was a success.

My beta test was scheduled to be performed on my birthday, April 18, 2010. I was over the moon when I found this out! I thought

God would be giving me my best birthday present ever! There was no other explanation. After all we had been through, I couldn't imagine a better ending than being told I was pregnant on my birthday!

Unexplicably, the beta results came back showing I wasn't pregnant. God must have felt horrible knowing how the beta result would make me feel. God must have known my faith would be tested when I heard the worst news I could ever imagine on my birthday.

The transfer was not successful.

That was the hardest time I had gone through. I didn't imagine or believe I could survive that pain. We were devastated beyond words. I would love to tell you that I trusted God, put all my faith in Him, knew it would all be okay, and He had a plan. But I didn't. I admit I was disappointed in God. I was angry. I just couldn't understand why we had to go through so much struggle and pain. First we had to go through the transplant and all Mark's health issues. Now we were dealing with infertility and with this horrible loss. Why were we struggling so much? Were we being punished or tested? It was hard to lean on God. We felt lost.

After the transfer in Michigan didn't work, we talked to our local doctor about our next step. He told us we could get on a list for donated embryos at our clinic. We had some hope when we heard about this list. However, we were told the wait was at least two years long. Our hearts sank. We couldn't wait that long. It didn't cost anything to get on the list, so we went ahead and put our names on it. We thought it wouldn't hurt to be on it.

Knowing we were running out of options, we started a lengthy, drawn out adoption process in the summer of 2010. I admit that my heart wasn't completely in it. As much as I desperately wanted to be a mom, I still desired to be pregnant, too. I just wasn't ready to let the dream go.

Then, in December 2010, something happened that we could later only describe as a "God thing". We received an email from our clinic stating there were donated embryos available for us. A two-year wait had turned into a six-month answer to prayer.

We were shocked, excited, and filled with hope!

We put the adoption process on hold and prepared for another frozen embryo transfer. Like the previous transfer, we had three embryos available to us. Although they weren't the same quality as the previous embryos, they were still "good" quality. This time, however, we would be able to do the transfer at our clinic because the embryos were stored at our clinic. We didn't need to travel to another state. We would also be able to do the transfer and blood work all in the comfort of our own clinic. Things were looking good, and we were grateful to God for another opportunity to become pregnant.

During the first embryo transfer, the devastation of one embryo not surviving the thaw seemed to overshadow the transfer of the other two embryos. I honestly didn't expect it to be that hard for me. I felt like it took away a lot of the miracle of the embryos that did survive and were transferred into me. I knew most likely the transfer I was about to undergo was going to be my last chance at becoming pregnant. I wanted to enjoy as much of the experience as I could. I went into this transfer with a different mindset. I was going to focus on the embryos that survived and that miracle and not the loss of an embryo if that was the case.

Just prior to the transfer, the doctor came in with the same news I had heard before, "We had to thaw all three. One embryo didn't survive." But this time, I smiled and rejoiced. I was about to be pregnant with twins! While I also grieved the one that didn't survive, I turned my focus to the ones that did survive. I felt blessed and grateful.

The transfer dates were ironically so close to the previous dates of the transfer the year before. When I asked when the beta test would be following the transfer, the nurse nonchalantly said, "I think we will schedule it for April 18."

My birthday. The beta test was once again scheduled on my birthday.

I got really quiet. The nurse asked me if that would work out. I remember whispering, "Yes, that will be fine." Truth be told, I was overwhelmed with crushing distress. I wondered if it was a cruel joke God was playing on me. How could He do this to me? Two years in a row? And on my birthday?

Then, my attitude turned a complete 180 degrees. Wait a minute. Hello! This just had to work. The test had to be positive. After all, God would never allow that to happen again. Would He? That would just be too much. Was this a way to "redeem" Himself in my eyes? Return my faith and trust in Him?

The dreaded two-week wait never felt longer than those particular two weeks. I experienced profoundly tumultuous emotions ranging from being excited to scared to nervous to hopeful and doubtful. A true whirlwind of emotions.

On the morning of April 18, 2011, I was scheduled to have my beta test. I decided I needed to mentally prepare myself for what the test would say. I decided to do a home pregnancy test. After I had peed on the stick, I was so nervous that I couldn't look at the result of the test. Mark had to look at it.

"What does it say, Mark?" He didn't say anything.

I sighed. "Is it negative?"

He nodded slightly. "Yeah, I think so."

My heart dropped, and I sighed deeply. I went to grab the test out of his hands so I could throw it against the wall, rip it apart, or something violent.

But then I looked at it. There were two lines.

"Mark, it's positive! It's not negative! It's positive!"

"Really? But it's not a dark line."

"It doesn't matter, honey! A line is a line! It's positive!"

For years, we had tested with ovulation prediction kits where we were looking for a dark line and the darker the line the better. Mark assumed the pregnancy test would be the same, and he was looking for a line that was just as dark as the other line.

Seeing that second line was something I will never forget. I started crying. "Mark, it's positive! Oh my goodness! I'm pregnant!" We hugged, and Mark smiled so big! He said seeing my happiness was something he would never forget.

My mom worked a couple blocks away from our house, and I wanted to surprise her. I had told everyone I wasn't going to test early. I was just going to wait for the blood test. So, I knew she wouldn't be expecting me, and I wanted her to be the first to know.

Walking into her office with a pee stick in my hand was a bit awkward. Not too many people walk into an office holding a stick they peed on. But it was an exhilarating feeling. I'll never forget the look on my mom's face when I showed her the stick and said, "It's positive!" She had tears in her eyes as she hugged me and said, "Oh I'm so happy! I didn't know what we were going to do if it was negative."

Of course I had to call my dad right away too. I called him from my mom's office as she snapped a picture. Telling my parents that they were going to be grandparents was the best experience.

Next I went to my closest friend April's house to show her the test. She had walked this journey with us from the very beginning, and I wanted her to know next. She had begged me not to test and had encouraged me to wait for the blood test. She wanted me to enjoy the knowledge that I was indeed pregnant until proven otherwise. I knocked on her door with the pregnancy test in my hand. When she answered the door, I showed it to her and said, "I didn't listen to you!" She looked at the test, screamed, and hugged me tight. It was an amazing feeling. I had waited years for this moment, and I was going to enjoy every second.

Even though I had taken a home pregnancy test, and it was positive, I still had to go in for the beta test. The beta test is a blood test that would give a more accurate reading about the pregnancy and the level of hormones in my body.

I had my blood drawn and waited for my doctor to call to tell me what the number was. I knew it was going to be positive, and

I was going to have a number, but I was anxious to hear what the number was.

I had worked with my doctor for years during our infertility journey. She had performed all twelve IUIs each with disappointing results. I think it was an exciting moment for both of us when she was able to tell me, "Tammy! You're pregnant! Congratulations!" It was a moment which we had been waiting for years. I asked her what the number was, and she told me it was eighteen. I was a bit surprised that it was that low, but she reassured me that every pregnancy is different and every woman is different. It wasn't about the number, but whether it increased or decreased as time went on. I felt much better and relished in the fact that I was pregnant, and I had received the news on my birthday! I finally got to see those two lines on the pee stick that many other women get to see. I finally got a positive beta test. God answered my prayers! It was a dream come true!

I'll never forget the moments of that birthday in 2011. Never. I was floating on air. It was the best birthday ever, and I still hold onto that dear memory. For the next two days, life had never been better. I was excited to be pregnant. Those two days were amazing.

Our doctor wanted to check the beta levels every two days to make sure the levels were increasing. Ideally, they like to see the beta level double in forty-eight hours. I went in for another beta test on April 20, two days after my positive test. I honestly had no worries. I felt good, and I was on cloud nine. Mark and I were betting on what the number would be.

We wanted a level of at least thirty-two. My heart dropped when I found out the level was eight. I was miscarrying. I would no longer be pregnant.

I got the call from the doctor at home. I got off the phone and went down the hall to tell Mark. I didn't have to say a word. I collapsed to the floor in grief and in tears. Mark came running to me and held me as I sobbed. He knew the news wasn't good. My almost three-year-old niece was also at our house. She knew we were hoping to get a call saying her cousin was growing. When she saw me crying, she asked if her cousin was in Heaven. Through tears, I said yes. She rubbed my back and said, "I really wanted a cousin." We were all grieving deeply. It was too hard to understand. Too hard for me to process. Too hard for me to accept.

I spent days in bed. I would like to say I trusted in God, and believed He had a plan, but I didn't. I admit I was incredibly angry with Him. There were times I would shake my fist at Heaven and say, "Don't make me come up there!" I just couldn't begin to understand how He could do this to us. We had already been through so much. Why? Why us?

After a few days of laying in bed and crying, I finally prayed to God, "God, I can't do this anymore. All I want to do is crawl into a hole and never come back up. I need You to help me. I need Your strength to get me out of this bed and keep going." It was only then that I could finally slowly get up and move ahead. Things didn't magically get better. Some days I considered it a success if I was able to get up and get dressed. I cried many tears for months and grieved greatly. But God gave me the strength to keep going when I asked Him to.

I knew this was my last chance to be pregnant. I knew it in my heart. I knew if I wanted to be a mom, we needed to move onto the next step--adoption. For the longest time I couldn't understand why God would allow me to be pregnant and then take it away. I wanted to be pregnant so bad and carry my baby.

But as time went on, when I did ask God, "Why didn't you answer my prayer?", I would hear Him tell me, "I did." I prayed to God to allow me to be pregnant. I wanted to see that positive pregnancy test. I wanted to be able to rub my stomach and know there was a life inside of me. And that's exactly what happened. I was pregnant. I saw the positive pregnancy test. For two wonderful days, I knew I had a life inside of me and possibly two lives inside of me. He answered my prayer. It may not have been the way I wanted or thought I needed, but He did answer my prayer. I will always be grateful to God for my beautiful experience. I can say I was pregnant with twins.

CHAPTER 7

FROM INFERTILITY TO ADOPTION

It was weeks before I felt we could move to the next step in our journey to have a baby. Still, I admit it wasn't easy. The next step was adoption, but I had to grieve the loss of not carrying my baby. It truly was a loss that I had to accept and grieve before I could move forward. I wanted to be mentally prepared when we started the adoption process. I wanted to be 100 percent in it, not anything less.

I took the time to cry, to be angry, and just "be me". I struggled to understand why I couldn't have one simple wish—to carry my baby. It didn't seem like a big thing to ask. So why couldn't I have that? It just wasn't fair. There were times I felt betrayed by God. I would shake my fist at the sky and say, "Just You wait until I get up there. You have some explaining to do!" I would cry in the shower as it was easier to cry in there. I was getting wet anyway and the sound of the shower drowned out the sound of my crying. I admit that it took me awhile not to feel angry at God. I felt like He was taking a precious gift away from me—the gift of carrying a child.

While others tried to encourage me and help me "get through it", I knew only I could truly help myself. I needed to move ahead in my own time, at my own pace, and in my own way. I truly appreciated all the support and love people showed me. I couldn't have gotten through it without their support. But I couldn't move forward until I knew I was ready, and I didn't want to rush into it.

Moving forward was a process that took time. Slowly the anger and sadness lessened. It never went away completely and some days it would creep back in. But I knew over time those strong negative feelings were lessening, and the feeling of hope was creeping back in. I couldn't rush it, though. I wanted to move forward with the adoption process having grieved appropriately and be fully invested in it.

At the same time, I truly felt God had a plan. My desire to be a mom was still there even if my dream of being pregnant didn't seem possible. I prayed to God every day if I wasn't meant to be a mom, please take the desire away from my heart. The desire didn't go away, and in fact, just kept getting stronger.

In the summer 2011, I felt I was ready to start the adoption process.

I often get asked how we got approved to adopt considering Mark's health issues. I can understand their curiosity because he was so sick. My answer is always the same, "It was God." I never in my wildest dreams thought we would be approved to adopt. In fact, I had asked several people who had gone through a home study and they confirmed my impression--Mark would never pass the health exam.

A fellow blogger, who had health issues and had adopted a baby girl, emailed me shortly after I miscarried in the spring 2011. She wanted to help. She asked if she could email her adoption consultant to see about any recommendations or if she could help us. I told her that would be great, although in my mind I knew it would be a dead end. I thought she was a sweet friend who was trying to help. I will forever be grateful to this friend because God used her to open the doors for us.

I was surprised when I got an email from her consultant saying that she could email a few agencies in Wisconsin to see if any would work with us. I appreciated her help, so of course I said she could.

I was still expecting this to be a dead end. Thankfully, instead of a dead end, we actually had choices.

Seriously?! Choices? "Could this be true?" I asked myself.

She found several agencies willing to work with us. She clarified that just because Mark had health issues, it didn't automatically disqualify us. My heart sank a little when I found out he still would need to pass a health exam and get a letter from his doctor. We probably had a better chance of getting struck by lightning than having Mark pass a health exam. But at this point we had nothing to lose. I knew if we didn't at least try, we would always wonder "what if".

I called the agency the consultant recommended, and we set up an interview. I thought we would be throwing away the $2000 down payment for the consultation, but again, we wanted to do everything we could to have a child.

The health exam wasn't as detailed as I had feared. It was just a simple exam. But, it would be an exam just the same. Our social worker said she needed a letter explaining Mark's diagnosis, his life expectancy, how he was doing, and if he could care for a child.

Most people stress about their house during a home study, the finances, or something else. There is always something to stress about. The only thing I was completely and totally stressed about was Mark passing this health exam and how this letter was going to affect our chances to adopt.

We had a close relationship with Mark's doctor. I guess years of being a patient will do that to you. We probably saw his doctor more than we saw our families. He knew our struggle with infertility. He also knew we were trying to adopt. I knew he would gladly write the letter for us. When I explained what they needed in the letter and they needed to know Mark's life expectancy, he rolled his eyes and said, "Don't they realize that nothing is guaranteed and even you, Tammy, could die tomorrow?"

Well, now that's comforting.

In all seriousness, he did a fantastic job writing the letter and explaining things. A big sigh of relief.

That is, until we were told we would also need a letter from Mark's kidney doctor.

At this point I was a bit frustrated. Mark saw several different types of doctors including a cardiologist, neurologist, kidney transplant doctor, etc. I thought we were going to keep going around in circles, needing more and more letters. But the social worker assured me that all she needed was one from his kidney doctor with answers to the same questions.

This letter made me more nervous. Even though we were friendly with our kidney doctor, we weren't nearly as close to him as Mark's primary doctor. He had no idea about our infertility journey or our need to adopt. I thought he would laugh in our faces and think we were out of our minds for even thinking of adoption. But actually the opposite was true. When I called to ask him for the letter, he was thrilled for us and honored to write a letter. He asked questions and really wanted to know how things were going. We got tremendous support from him and it was encouraging. The letter he wrote was touching and heartfelt. I cried reading it. He had wonderful things to say about both of us and stated Mark was doing a wonderful job taking care of himself.

I knew then that we could pass the health examination without a problem. Doors were opening up and just when I thought they would close, God kept opening them.

We went through the seemingly never-ending process of a home study. There was so much to think about and do. There was paperwork upon paperwork to do, background check after background check. We felt like we were telling our deepest secrets and fears to a social worker who was a complete stranger. They really put you through the ringer when you want to adopt a child. I'm surprised they didn't need to my know cousin's ex-wife's daughter's dog's blood type.

It was not only a lot of paperwork and interviews, but it was also very expensive. We had already spent about $30,000 on infertility treatment with the IUIs, IVF, and the two embryo transfers. I was extremely fortunate that I was working from home, and I was able to work as much overtime as I wanted. It was a true blessing to be able to afford our infertility treatments. Without being able to work overtime, it would have been impossible. I was working about sixty hours a week. I was also coaching gymnastics to earn even more money. Mark and I were selling toy cars and baby blankets at craft and toy shows in our area to earn money. We were doing everything we could to raise money for the adoption.

When an adoption "situation" is presented to potential adoptive parents, the cost could be as little as $15,000 or as much as $75,000 or more depending on the situation. As part of the home study, we were required to determine our budget for what we could afford for an adoption situation. This was to make sure we could financially pay for the initial adoption fees, support taking care of the baby, and to be sure we wouldn't begin raising a baby with too much debt. When you're faced with an adoption opportunity, your heart wants a baby at any cost and you will do anything to take a baby home. Obviously, this isn't the smartest way to approach raising a child. So by having a budget, we figured out whether to move forward and accept an adoption. After going through our financial records, we determined our budget was $50,000. This was the most we could afford while still being financially stable enough to take care of a baby after the adoption.

It took about five months to get all the paperwork and required tests done. When we were finally given the green light to submit our profiles to birth mothers to consider us as parents, we were excited. A profile is a book of information and pictures of us and our families so birth mothers can get to know us better. This helps her to be able to make an informed decision. I can't imagine being in a birth mother's shoes and making such an important decision. By providing a profile, birth mothers can learn more about potential adoptive parents.

We hired a consultant through Christian Adoption Consultants.

Through this company, we were exposed to more adoption situations. We also determined if we wanted our profile submitted to any particular birth mother. We were given just a little bit of information about the birth mother, the sex of the baby, and the cost of that particular adoption. If we were interested, we would tell the agency that they could present our profile to the birth mother as potential adoptive parents for consideration.

We submitted our profile to seven different birth mothers within a month, but none of the birth mothers chose us. It was hard to remain focused and not become discouraged. We continued to pray, but there were many days we felt little hope. We felt like doors were opening only to have them close again over and over, and it didn't feel good at all.

Then we were informed about a situation which sounded promising. A birth mother, with no health concerns, was pregnant with a baby girl. The total cost would be about $60,000, which was $10,000 over our budget. Regretfully, we asked our profile not be submitted. They emailed to confirm we didn't want our profile submitted. This is common practice to confirm they were doing precisely what we requested. We confirmed "We do not want our profile to be submitted."

It was a couple weeks later that we received an email from our agency saying the birth mother had chosen us.

Huh? We were confused. We couldn't figure out what had happened. How could a birth mother choose us when we hadn't submitted our profile? I sat at the computer reading that email over and over: *You guys were chosen! I'll contact you in the morning to discuss the next steps! Congratulations!*

I felt glued to my chair. What do I do? Who do I contact? Was this a joke? Was I reading it correctly?

I forwarded the email to our consultant to make sure I was reading it correctly and that we were chosen. It sure sounded like we were. There weren't too many ways to misinterpret that, but I just didn't know what to think at that time. She emailed me right back stating that it sure sounded like we had been chosen and congratulated us. This was surreal and too confusing, so I gave her a call and said something wasn't right. After explaining our confirmed email, our consultant was stunned. She really wasn't sure what was going on and wanted to do some checking into the situation. She was just as surprised as I was.

Eventually we determined the agency had accidentally submitted our profile to this birth mother after we had asked them not to. When I heard that, my heart sank. I thought for sure the agency would take the baby away because there was an error. I thought because it was over our budget, they would say we couldn't accept the baby. The agency felt awful about the mistake and then asked if we were still interested. Of course we were still interested! Honestly, the minute the agency said we could still be considered as adoptive parents, there was no way we were going to say no. We knew this was our daughter, and we were going to bring her home.

But we were faced with a big problem. We needed to come up with an additional $10,000 in one month's time, and it was almost Christmas. The baby's due date was December 27, 2011.

Yikes! We didn't know how to raise that much money in such a short time. There were no sources of money we hadn't already tapped. We had already taken out all the equity in our home, and we couldn't get loans due to Mark's disability. We honestly had no idea. It seemed hopeless.

But we also believed there was a reason our profile was accidentally submitted. We knew this baby girl was our daughter. We could have refused this adoption, but in our hearts we knew this was no mistake. God brought this little girl to us. We had to put our trust in Him.

But, $10,000 in one month and at Christmas? The end of the year normally was hard enough financially for us due to Christmas and big health deductibles in January. Trying to earn the additional $10,000 seemed to be a mountain far too big to climb. I would love to be able to say we had the faith of a grain of mustard seed and we were able to move that mountain. But, I admit, I sincerely had my doubts.

What seemed impossible to us turned out to be a miracle from God. Our church reached out to us to see if they could host a benefit for us. They had a silent auction full of many items that were generously donated from local businesses. Ladies from our church baked pies to auction off. They had a chili supper and bake sale. Many friends and family came and also donated to the benefit. People who I had met through blogging all over the world donated. We felt an amazing amount of love and support. We couldn't believe it when the total amount was almost exactly what we needed. To. The. Dollar.

It was even more of a confirmation that this baby was meant to be our daughter.

The day after the benefit, we traveled to Utah where our daughter would be born. The plan was to induce the birth mother a week prior to the due date so we could be there for the delivery.

On December 19, 2011, we met the birth mother for the first time. I was a bundle of nerves. I don't think nervous is a strong enough word to convey my emotions. I was about to meet the woman who was entrusting me to be the mother of the baby she was carrying. How could I meet the expectations of someone so incredible?

I walked into the restaurant and to the table that was reserved for us. When the birth mother stood up and turned around to me, I was in awe. She was absolutely beautiful. Then I saw her perfectly round stomach.

Our baby. My first look at our baby.

I couldn't help but tear up as I walked toward her. I wrapped my arms around her and the first words she said to me were, "I'm not gonna lie. I'm so nervous I feel like I'm going to puke!" I laughed and said, "Oh, me too!" We both laughed at that moment and I instantly relaxed.

We talked all during dinner. We wanted to get to know her,

and she wanted to get to know us. After awhile I looked at the birth mother and asked her the question I was dying to know, "Why did you choose us, especially with all of Mark's health issues?"

She smiled, and I'll never forget her words. "Tammy, Mark's health issues is exactly why I chose you guys. I have been through a lot in my life. When I was reading the profiles, you guys really stood out to me. I knew you were the ones. You've been through so much, and you remind me of me. I wanted to give this baby to you guys because you deserve a child, and you need to know good things do happen."

Wow. The main reason we thought would hinder us in being chosen was the exact reason we were chosen. It reminded us of the cornerstone in the Bible. Builders had rejected and threw away the very rock that became the chief cornerstone. The suffering and heartache we wanted to hide away from became the fundamental reason we were chosen.

The birth mother's induction was scheduled for the next morning. We had to be at the hospital at six in the morning. I was a ball of emotions that morning. Scared, excited, nervous, and feeling like I was going to hurl my dinner everywhere.

It was a long day. Her labor wasn't progressing as it should and at one point, she was in a lot of pain. I came to her side, gave her a hug, and said, "I'm so sorry. I would trade places with you if I could." Through a grimace she said, "Oh, I know you would."

She got it. She understood. Mother to mother, I felt like we really understood each other's feelings.

The doctor was evaluating whether or not to proceed with a C-section when finally the birth mother dilated enough to start pushing. We were all relieved that a C-section wasn't going to be necessary. I held onto the birth mother's leg as she pushed. I had never seen a baby being born. It was incredible. Not only was I watching a baby being born, but I was watching <u>my</u> baby being born. I watched with tears in my eyes as I saw the first hint of fine, baby hair. Her small head started emerging, followed by a pink little body tucked into a tight, tiny ball.

Suddenly, she was here. I had never seen a more beautiful, brown-eyed, brown-haired, tiny baby. For the second time in two days I stood in absolute awe. I couldn't help shedding tears as I heard her first cry.

On December 20, 2011 at 4:45 p.m., Hannah Dawn Wondra came into the world.

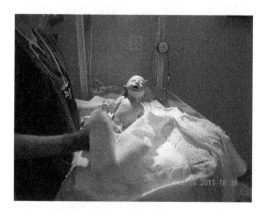

Hannah's first picture

I had the joy and privilege of being the first one to hold Hannah. That was something that was important to Hannah's birth mother. She wanted the baby to know me first. That was an amazing and selfless act. It showed how much she really loved this baby and wanted what was best for the baby. That was something I cherished. I'll never forget the moment when they put her in my arms and tears of happiness formed in my eyes as I looked at Hannah's perfect, beautiful face. It was just how I had imagined. It was such a perfect moment.

But then I looked up. Hannah's birth mother's eyes filled with tears for a very different reason. As she said, "Merry Christmas Tammy and Mark", she started sobbing. Suddenly, my tears of joy were replaced with her heartbreak. I whispered "I'm so sorry" to her as we shared the pain of her loss, together. My perfect moment and elation was now also breaking my heart. I have never felt such strong emotions at the same time and on such different ends of the spectrum.

I was filled with mixed emotions that whole day. The day your child is born is supposed to be the happiest day of your life, but it was also very sad for me.

I know I was one of the lucky adoptive moms who was fortunate to be in the delivery room when her baby was born. Not all birth mothers are that understanding and accommodating. She even let my mom be in the delivery room which was truly amazing. She was open to having anyone we wanted in the delivery room, and that was a gift I didn't take for granted. We were blessed. I was able to feel Hannah kick her birth mother, which was a moment I'll never forget. I was able to hear Hannah's heartbeat on the monitor. I was able to hold the birth mother's leg as she pushed Hannah into this world. I was the one who cut Hannah's umbilical cord. The hospital allowed me to do all the first-time mother things, and I was fortunate we had such an amazing birth mother who let me do those things. I was able to give Hannah her first bath. Many adoptive mothers don't get that opportunity and I did. I feel blessed and honored I was able to experience that.

Despite all of these blessings and being able to do all the "firsts", it never really felt like I was Hannah's mother when she was born. This was because in the hospital, birth mothers still retain all rights. Even though the papers had been signed by the birth mother terminating her rights, all decisions were up to the birth mother as long as she was in the hospital. We couldn't see Hannah in the nursery unless the birth mother said it was okay. Of course she always let us see Hannah whenever we wanted to. The birth mother made the choices in regards to getting pictures done, when to feed her, whether or not to introduce her to a pacifier, etc. It wasn't a big deal when looking at the big picture, but it was not how I expected to be treated in the hospital.

Suddenly, I was grieving a different loss. I wanted to be back in Wisconsin, recovering, having my doctor deliver my baby. I wanted to have that precious experience with her. I didn't want to be states away watching another woman give birth to my baby. I wanted things different. The first time my closest family met Hannah was Skyping twenty-four hours after she was born when we became her legal guardians. We had to Skype sitting next to the birth mother. Despite wanting to shout to the world that Hannah was our daughter, I had to refrain any excitement as I didn't want to hurt the birth mother. I wanted to respect her feelings.

It wasn't an easy situation at all.

When Hannah was born and I wanted to start nursing her right away (yes, it's possible to induce lactation), the hospital wouldn't let me until the birth mother and Hannah were released. I'll never forget when one nurse said to me, "Until they are released from the hospital, the baby isn't yours." She pointed to another nurse and said, "It would be like letting her nurse the baby if we let you nurse her."

I wanted to scream, "No it's not like that at all! I'm Hannah's mother!"

The birth mother experienced some complications and needed to spend an extra night in the hospital. Despite the fact that we had already signed the placement papers and the birth mother had terminated her rights, we still had no rights. The first official night as a family of three, my mom, Mark, and I spent the night in the hospital waiting room. Our daughter was sleeping in the nursery, rooms away. We had the option of going home, but I was adamant that I was not going to leave our daughter no matter what.

I admit, it was hard. I was caught off guard with how different everything was for adoptive parents. It was definitely surreal. I expected the fairy tale vision: We would have the perfect delivery. The baby would be passed to me. I would immediately feel the bond between my daughter and me. Tears of happiness would flow from my eyes. We would sign the papers twenty-four hours later, and we would happily leave the hospital, just like any other parents would. Yes, I knew it would be hard on the birth mother, and I knew I would feel sadness for her. But honestly, I never realized how much the whole process would affect me. I would never have guessed the roller coaster of emotions I would feel. It was nothing like I dreamed it would be.

It reminds me of another woman's birth story.

+ + ◆ ◆ + +

When I think about how Hannah came into this world, I can't help but think of Mary when she gave birth to Jesus. Here she was, about to give birth to God's son. She is riding on a donkey into a crowded town with no room available in an inn, much less a hospital. She gave birth in a stable. Her baby was placed in a manger of hay. Obviously, it was nothing like she expected.

I don't know what Mary was thinking, but I'm sure she was panicking when she heard there were no rooms available in Bethlehem. She must have been in so much pain from the labor. I'm sure she was terrified about having a baby without any help or comforts of home.

And yet, her experience was uniquely God's plan.

Do I wish my experience bringing my daughter into this world was different? Absolutely. Mary was probably thinking the same thing, and I'm sure at times she felt forgotten by God. Couldn't He have made it easy for her? I mean, she WAS carrying the Son of God. He certainly deserved better than being born in a stable.

I'm sure Mary also felt like she couldn't do it, and she felt the weight of the world on her shoulders. While I certainly didn't have the weight of the world on my shoulders, I did feel the pressure of not letting Hannah's birth mother down. I didn't want to fail her. After all, she was giving me my daughter to raise and trusting me with something that was huge and such a big responsibility. Letting her down wasn't even an option for me.

I believe that was how Mary felt. She wasn't going to let God down. Failure was not an option.

No one will ever forget the way Jesus came into this world. It is definitely not the way you expect the Son of God to come into this world.

But, it's not how you come into this world, it's the impact you have on this world.

God blessed me by giving me more opportunities than most adoptive parents. So I was disturbed and shocked at the negative feelings I felt. Was I being ungrateful? Was I letting Him down because I felt these frustrated and negative feelings?

God proved to me that He understood. In time, I understood the fullness of His plan. Although it wasn't the way I wanted or expected, I was able to be there for Hannah's birth mother. I was able to see firsthand the true loss she felt and comfort her. My heart was more open to the hard part of the adoption process---the part that seldom is ever talked about. The part that I can talk about and share with other adoptive moms to better prepare them.

God had planned how my daughter would come into this world. It was not in a way that I was expecting. I definitely didn't prefer it, but it ended up being just what was needed for me, for the birth mother, and potentially other adoptive moms.

It wasn't easy, but I'm honored God chose me to see His works and be a part of His plan. It may not be my idea of the perfect situation, but it is His.

———— ✦✦✦✦✦ ————

In Utah, twenty-four hours after giving birth, the birth mother as the option to sign her rights over to the adoptive parents. Believe it or not, twenty-four hours is actually a short amount of time. Some states give the birth mother a month or even three months. This was one of the reasons we had chose to adopt in Utah. We didn't want to be in a situation where the birth mother could change her mind months after we had the baby.

It was the longest twenty-four hours of my life. She could easily change her mind. She didn't have to sign the papers if she didn't want to. When it came to the twenty-four-hour mark, Hannah's birth mother went into one room and we went into another. I was really nervous and scared. What if she changed her mind? She had never given us any indication that she would change her mind, but we knew she had every right to. She easily could, no questions asked.

We signed our papers and waited for the social worker to come into the room. She came in after briefly meeting with the birth mother and said, "Congratulations!" It was that moment that I could breathe again. Hannah was our baby. Her birth mother had signed her rights over to us. The long twenty-four-hour wait was over.

What should have been an entirely happy moment was actually also quite sad for me. While I certainly was happy, I couldn't help but think of the birth mother and what she was going through. The thought made me so sad, and I just sat there and cried. I put my hands over my face as the tears fell onto my hands. I cried tears of not only sadness, but also of relief and happiness. I was feeling a variety of emotions all at the same time, and it was overwhelming.

Mark put his arm around my shoulders and held me until the tears subsided. The social worker let us stay in the room until I composed myself. I didn't want to go back to the birth mother's room until I was in better control of my emotions. After all, she was already going through so much. I wanted to be strong for her. But my heart was broken for her and the hard decision she had just made.

Later, I went into the nursery and held Hannah as I was feeding her. I was still emotional, mostly such sadness for the birth mother. I had gotten to know her very well. I didn't want to see her going through such heartache. A nurse came up to me and said, "It is so touching that you are feeling sad for the birth mother, but you also need to be happy for you. It's really okay to be happy. She wants you to be happy. She chose you guys because she knows you'll be great parents. You owe it to her and to yourself to be happy."

Easier said than done, but she opened my eyes. She helped me to realize I did need to be happy not only for myself but also for the birth mother. Thanks to the words of that nurse, I was able to relax more and focus on the miracle of the gift of my daughter.

The next day we spent the whole day with Hannah's birth mother, her son, and her boyfriend. We talked and laughed. Because she was still in the hospital, we weren't allowed to take Hannah home. The rules were that a social worker had to be there as long as we were together. So during that day, a social worker was also in the hospital room with us. The social worker was amazed at the connection we had. She said she had seen a lot of adoptions but ours was the most unusual because of the strong connection we had to each other.

The next day the birth mother was discharged which meant we were finally able to bring our baby girl home. While I was packing up our stuff, I was a ball of emotions. After spending two full days with Hannah's birth mother and forming a connection few would ever understand, I was sad to be saying goodbye to her.

We got Hannah strapped into our car, and I turned around to say goodbye to the birth mother. She had tears in her eyes as she gave me the biggest hug. With her arms tightly wrapped around me, she whispered, "Take good care of her." I whispered back my vow, "I will. I promise." It was hard to do with the big lump in my throat. Even though we have talked a couple times on the phone since, that moment was the last time I saw her.

*Our first family picture taken the day we brought
Hannah home from the hospital*

The next hurdle involved the wait for clearance from Wisconsin in order to come home with Hannah. It usually takes just a few days, but since it was the holiday season, we were told we probably wouldn't get clearance to come home until after the New Year. We were crushed. We wanted to get home, especially since it was the holidays. But we prepared our hearts to spend Christmas away from our families. We already had the best gift of all, our daughter.

You can imagine the surprise when less than twenty-four hours after signing the papers we got the call from our social worker saying, "I think you guys broke a record in being the fastest to be cleared. Everything went through! You guys are free to go home!" Because it was the holidays they had sped up the process so we could be home for Christmas. We were so grateful and humbled. I know they were working hard and we were appreciative that they tried hard and succeeded to get the clearance to go through as soon as possible.

On Christmas Day 2011, we spent the day traveling home from Utah to Wisconsin. My dad and sister picked us up from the airport. Their eyes lit up as they saw us walk through the gates of the terminal. They were meeting their granddaughter and niece for the very first time!

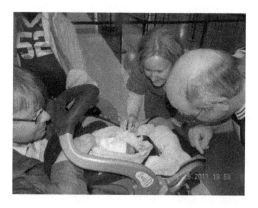

Bringing our daughter home on Christmas Day 2011

It was 9 p.m. on Christmas night and the Green Bay Packers were playing (our families are big Packers fans), so we didn't expect to come home to a house with all the lights on, kids anxiously peeking out the windows and waving. What a wonderful surprise to see our families had come to welcome the newest member of the family to our home! With the football game on the television in the background, we all took turns gushing and holding our sweet Hannah until my exhaustion was evident to everyone in the room. They all left our home after giving big congratulatory hugs to Mark and me.

My mom helped us unpack our necessities quickly and got Hannah ready for bed. As I hugged and thanked my parents, saying goodbye as they walked out the door, I couldn't help but smile as I turned around after shutting and locking the door to find Mark holding a sleeping Hannah in his arms. I was exhausted from traveling all day, but seeing my husband with our precious daughter took my breath away.

+ + + + + +

I often think back to our journey of becoming parents.

What if our profile wouldn't have been submitted by mistake?

What if we would have said, "No, it's a mistake" after the birth mother chose us?

What if our family and friends wouldn't have come together and gave generously so we were able to raise $10,000 in just weeks?

The answer to those questions was always the same: It was never in our control.

God was the one who decided the profile would be submitted.

Three times God said, "Here is your daughter. There is no mistake."

God divinely intervened to raise $10,000 and open the hearts of many people who listened to the call of God.

When investigating how the "mistaken submission" happened in the agency, the worker reported I had called to explain that we had changed our minds and wanted our profile submitted to the birth mother. They insisted this "mistake" never happened. In all their years of adoptions, no one had ever submitted a profile to a birth mother accidentally.

I know I never made that phone call. I always preferred emailing as I wanted all communication in writing. To this day, I feel it was an angel who made that call.

From the time we started trying to have a baby in 2002 until Hannah was born in 2011, I prayed to God that He bless me in becoming a mother. I would take any child—just put one on the doorstep—I didn't care. I had secretly prayed for a girl who looked just like Mark.

Of all the miracles, the fact that Hannah looks completely like her father is the most remarkable. I can't tell you how many times I hear that Hannah looks exactly like her daddy. It has been a constant reminder to me that God answers prayers.

Hannah was meant to be our daughter. We had to cross many hurdles to bring her home and yet here she is today. It was always in His control and not ours.

One of the coolest things about our adoption story is an interesting fact I love to share.

Hannah's due date was December 27, 2011. Remember when we had our embryo transfer earlier in the year, and I received the positive pregnancy test? My due date would have been the same time as Hannah's birth. I believe when we got our positive pregnancy test, it was God's way of saying we would have a baby in nine months. Indeed we were "pregnant", just not in the way we thought. I remember sharing that tidbit with Hannah's birth mother and the nurse. They both wore shocked expressions on their faces. They couldn't believe the coincidence in how everything came to be.

God had it all planned out. He was letting us know we would have a baby. But at the time we didn't realize how our dream of a baby would come to be.

God can be sneaky like that.

CHAPTER 8

THE REASON BEHIND HANNAH'S NAME

I'd like to tell you about the woman whom our daughter was named after. She was the woman who gave me inspiration and strength. She struggled with many of the same emotions I felt, and I'm sure many of you have felt. Maybe you haven't felt it with infertility, but in other struggles of your life. Maybe a stressful job, a hard class, a failing relationship, being hurt by people in your life, or a different hardship.

Hannah was the fourth woman in the Bible to suffer with infertility. Sarah, Rebekah, Rachel, and Hannah all struggled with infertility. The difference between Hannah and the other three women was that she had faith and hope. The other three did not. Sarah laughed when she was told God would give her a child. Rebekah questioned God when her twins struggled in her womb. Rachel put the responsibility on her husband and was angry when she wasn't able to conceive.

But Hannah trusted God. She was an example of grace in the midst of grief. Through all the years of waiting and longing to be a mother, Hannah was devastated. She felt an incredible weight of grief. She wanted to be a mother desperately. The grief became unbearable at times, and she cried many tears. Her husband tried to comfort her in any way he could. He was also crushed at seeing her grief and not being able to help her. He insisted he loved her even if she couldn't give him children.

Hannah was emotionally exhausted from grief as months and months went by without becoming pregnant. I can imagine how she felt. Most likely she felt as though she had been sent on an endless journey into a huge desert without a map. No true end in sight. Always thirsty, always craving water and wanting more. Same thing over and over and never feeling like you're getting ahead. Just walking in the same cycle and craving the same thing over and over.

Endless and constant heartache.

Each time she thought she was finally starting to feel a little better, giving her a little more hope and encouragement, something would happen that would trip her up again.

And again and again.

Have you ever felt like that? Struggling and trying hard to move forward in a situation that seems you can never get ahead. I'm sure we can all relate to Hannah during tough times in our lives.

I can imagine the simplest things were hard for her. Hard to eat. Hard to drink. Why bother nourishing a body that continued to fail her over and over? She would try desperately to choke down a few bites just to make her husband happy, but swallowing past that hard knot in her throat was near impossible.

Finally, Hannah couldn't take any more. She went to the house of the Lord. With strength she didn't know she had, she went to the Lord. She didn't turn away from Him. She had never doubted her faith or God's plan, but that day, she stepped out in her faith like never before. She was determined to find peace. She knew she wasn't getting real answers to the difficulty getting pregnant, so she went straight to the Lord and took it up with Him.

In turning toward God to address her broken dreams and desperation, Hannah began to realize peace in letting go of her pain and in giving it to the Lord.

As Hannah approached to the house of the Lord, I'm sure she

was overcome with emotion. Her body shaking with silent sobbing while praying to the Lord to heal her broken body and heart. She desperately wanted to hear the name "Mommy". She wanted to be a mom more than anything else in the world.

Then she did something I cannot fathom. She promised to give her child back to the Lord in service to Him if He blessed her with a child.

Yes, that's right. She would give her child back to the Lord. She sacrificed both her heartache and future with the child to the Lord. Once she said that and made that promise, there was no turning back, and she knew it.

I desperately wanted to have that kind of faith and peace of mind. When I felt discouraged, laying in bed sobbing with the covers over my head, not being able to eat, angry at the situation, I thought of Hannah. She gave me hope and strength. I knew one day if we had a girl, I would name her Hannah. This woman of faith was the reason I was able to continue on with this journey, no matter how much heartache it entailed.

When Hannah left the temple that day, I know she left with a peace and renewed hope because she had placed her grief in the hands of God. But she also left not knowing how God would choose to answer her prayers. What a mix of emotions she must have felt. Hannah committed herself to God, what He thought was best for her and His will for her life.

God answered Hannah's prayer. He gave her a son whom she named Samuel which means "God has heard". She didn't forget the vow she made to the Lord.

I'm sure to Hannah, those years of waiting for a baby seemed so long but holding her son and spending those short months with her miracle son, flew by in the blink of an eye. She made a promise to the Lord. No matter how hard and painful it was, she was going to fulfill her promise. As a mother I can't imagine that journey to the temple when she gave her son back to the Lord to live at the temple. I can picture her clutching onto Samuel's hand so tight. I'm sure she worried how he would feel the first night in a new and strange place without her. As she left her son at the temple, I can't imagine the pain as she turned around and walked away. I'm sure there were tears once again. She had to deal with grief again.

But now it was for a different reason.

She knew she would need God's strength for the lonely walk home. After giving her child back to the Lord, the only person who could help her move forward was the Lord. She held onto the knowledge He had helped her survive her empty womb and trusted He would help her survive her empty arms once again.

Now THAT is a true step of faith.

As a mom, I can't imagine doing what she did. Hannah praised God for her blessing, and she kept her end of her vow. Talk about faith! God didn't forget her either. He blessed her with five more children after Samuel, and Hannah was granted the ability to visit her son once a year.

I'd like to say I was just like Hannah throughout our infertility journey, but I admit I wasn't. I was more like Sarah, Rebekah, and Rachel. I questioned. I got mad. I lost hope. But I would often think of Hannah and her faith and hope to trust in God again and again. Hannah inspired me to turn to God and turn to hope during our journey.

Having hope is a blessed thing. God wants us to have hope. Did you know that hope is mentioned 130 times in the King James Version of the Bible? Most people think hope is "hoping something will happen", but the biblical definition of hope is "confident expectation", an assurance regarding the things in our life that are unclear and unknown.

During our failed attempts and cycles during our infertility journey, I kept track of the number of days I had hope versus the number of days I felt utter despair. After a year of infertility treatments, I counted the days. During that year, I had 339 days of hope and 17 days of despair. That's a lot of hope. Some days I only had a little hope and other days a lot of hope, but there were many more days of hope than despair.

That's what God wants us to have---more hope than despair.

The journey of infertility was not a journey Hannah chose by any means. She was heartbroken, devastated, and depressed. But Hannah had no way of knowing God's ultimate plan was to bless her with a special son whom He would use to lead His people. In order to prepare Hannah's heart and the circumstances that would lead to Samuel to anoint Kings, heartache had to come first. God was preparing Hannah's heart so her son would be raised in a temple and bring a nation back to Him. Hannah knew none of this at the time. Had God given Hannah a child when she first desired motherhood, would she have ever dedicated Samuel to God? Probably not.

I went through a lot of grief and loss during our journey to have a baby. I have ten angel babies waiting for me in Heaven. I can't wait to see them, hold them, and tell them how much I love being their mother. But, at the same time, it's hard to not be their mother here on Earth. I grieve that. I think of my babies all the time. I wonder what they would look like, what their personalities would be like, would they be boys or girls. I miss them. I think about them all the time, just like any mother does for their children. Some days I miss them so much I can't stop the tears.

But I also know the loss I've felt and the grief I've gone through has been no accident. God has paved my way for my heart to become softer and more understanding for my daughter's sake. My heart was broken so I could help my daughter with her broken heart. I know when Hannah gets older, she'll have many questions. I know one day she will be sad and feel a loss for her birth mother. She may come to me with tears in my eyes and say, "Mom, I miss my birth mother." I'll cry with her and tell her that I'm sad too. We'll talk about how much her birth mother wanted her, how she didn't "give her up" and instead "gave her a better life". Hannah will know how much she loved (and loves) her enough to give her a more stable life. She will know she is blessed to have two mothers who love her so much while most people have only one. Would I be able to understand this if I hadn't struggled so much? Probably not.

Heartache had to come first for me, just like heartache had to come first for Hannah in the Bible.

God sees the big picture from beginning to end. We can only see the little piece right now. Our lives are like a big puzzle. Many pieces have to come together to make a masterpiece. Sometimes the pieces don't fit no matter how hard we try to make it work, and we have to try another piece. But God knows, and He is here to help us find the perfect piece.

One day Hannah will learn how she got her name. I hope and pray she will share the story with unstoppable love for God that will shine through and lead people to also know the love of God.

Just like the woman she was named after.

CHAPTER 9

LIFE AS A MOM

When we were going through the infertility treatments and adoption, people would tell me that after all we had gone through, when we did get our baby, we were going to be blessed with the best baby. They predicted the baby would hardly ever cry and would sleep perfectly through the night starting the day we came home from the hospital. We were going to have the perfect baby, they said.

I foolishly wholeheartedly believed them.

Life sure changed when Hannah was born. Our lives now revolved around Hannah. We were constantly feeding and changing diapers. We were exhausted. I did a lot of the caring for Hannah as Mark was obviously dealing with his own health issues. He couldn't get up at night when she cried because his eyesight was so poor. This was due to complications of his diabetes. His eyes had trouble adjusting to the light. It was too much of a risk for both Mark and Hannah as he could trip and fall while holding her. Therefore, it was always my responsibility to get up with her.

I had anticipated that. In fact, the social worker brought it up during our home study. She had asked me how I was going to handle doing most of the caring of the baby because Mark wouldn't be able to. I told her I was prepared to do it all. While I knew it was going to be hard, I also knew Mark would do what he could to help.

What I didn't anticipate was the months and months of the exhaustion.

Hannah was not an easy baby. She didn't like to sleep. We would joke, "I remember that time Hannah took a nap. It was the best hour of my life." She just wasn't a good sleeper. At night, she was up every two hours at least. I expected it for awhile but this went on for three months.

And then for several months after that. Followed by more months after that. It just didn't end. I was trembling and shaking with exhaustion.

I didn't feel I had any right to complain. After all, we had worked hard, spent a lot money, and went through much heartache. I finally got my baby. God gave me the baby I wanted desperately—a beautiful baby girl who looked like Mark. I should be cherishing every single second, even if it was hard. My love should be enough to keep this baby comforted. I felt guilty being tired. It was so hard. I had a lot of friends who were, and are, still waiting for their miracle.

I tried to put on a happy face and pretend it was all okay. Truth be told, I was exhausted. I tried everything under the sun to get Hannah to sleep. Everyone gave me their ideas. Some had the "magic trick". I would get frustrated when it would work for them but not for me.

I felt like a failure as a mom. What was I doing wrong? This can't be what others go through. I had a baby who I couldn't help get her to sleep. A "good" mom wouldn't be having this much trouble. I couldn't figure out what God was thinking when He gave me this baby. If I'm being honest, I was also angry at God for giving me a baby that required so much when I didn't have much to give in the first place. I would think to myself, *God, what are you trying to teach me? Never mind. I'm too exhausted to hear your message.* I struggled with depression. I questioned why I was a mother at all.

Finally, it was starting to take such a toll on me that I needed her babysitter to come and watch her more often. I felt like the baby was too much for me to handle. The thought of going to bed at night made me nauseous because I knew we were going to be up every couple hours. I hated nights. I had such anxiety going to bed.

People were leery to volunteer to take Hannah for the night so I could get some rest. I didn't blame them. People brought me meals to help which was a huge relief. I maybe lost out on sleep but at least I didn't have to cook.

When she was fifteen months old, I was at my wit's end. We took her to see a sleep specialist. They said she had severe separation anxiety. I was relieved to hear that there was something actually causing her to have sleeping issues. People would tell me that things would get better. I was given advice after advice. I think deep down I knew something wasn't right, and I was relieved when we got an answer.

We started co-sleeping. She still woke up every couple hours but it just took a little touch and a calming voice to get her to fall asleep. Many times I barely had to wake up, just reach over and comfort her. It was a game-changer!

I often think back to that time. It was such a hard time and not the experience I wanted to have as a new mom. I wanted the "perfect" baby experience. I wanted my baby to sleep through the night and only cry when she was hungry, wet, or tired. I knew few people had those experiences, and I desperately wanted that. I wanted to be able to concentrate on the love and blessing of our daughter and not focus on how burned out I was.

But I also knew that Hannah would be an only child. Having another baby or going through another adoption wouldn't be an option. Our home study only approved us for one baby and it was documented as such in our file. Because Hannah was a difficult baby and I was so exhausted, the craving for another baby wasn't strong anymore. If she had been the "perfect" baby like I planned, not being able to adopt another baby would have been torture to accept. Now my heart was content with one baby, and I truly believe going through that experience helped my heart. I'm thankful to God for diminishing my desire for another baby. Even though it was tough at the time, I believe it was a blessing.

Like Laura Story sings in her song, "Blessings", sometimes our blessings come through raindrops. I'm grateful for my raindrops. My raindrops felt more like a monsoon, but I'm still grateful for the rainbow they were working to produce.

CHAPTER 10

STRUGGLES WITH INFLUENZA AND A TRAUMATIC BRAIN INJURY

February 2014 was a month I wish I could forget.

It started out with Hannah being diagnosed with pneumonia and influenza B. She was only two years old. Then I started having influenza-like symptoms. I just knew I had influenza. So, knowing I was going to just get sicker, I hurried to do some quick food shopping to make sure we had plenty of food for Mark and Hannah. Yep, mom/wife mode kicked in big time. Shopping with influenza.

The next day's lab test confirmed I had influenza B.

You can guess what happened next. Despite all our attempts to keep him protected, Mark caught influenza. What is sad to me now is knowing I felt miserable with influenza, but Mark didn't even know he had it because he always felt that sick. I only knew he was sick because I saw the tremors in his hands were much worse than normal. I knew that happened when his immune system was down. It was hard to imagine Mark felt that sick and miserable all the time that he didn't even know he was sick with something as serious as influenza.

I brought him into the ER and he was promptly admitted. He was hospitalized because his health conditions made him vulnerable to severe and sudden medical problems. Even knowing this, nothing could have prepared me for what happened on February 14, two days after admission.

After work, I arrived at his hospital room for our evening visit. He was unresponsive and his left side was shaking uncontrollably! I screamed for help and suddenly a code blue was called.

Mark was having seizures. He was intubated and sent down to the Twin Cities for higher care. He remained unresponsive.

I was still sick with influenza myself. I was confined to Mark's ICU room, wearing a mask at all times. I was miserable, sitting on an uncomfortable chair all day, staring at machines. I was praying and hoping Mark could soon breathe on his own. I couldn't even leave the room to eat. I had to rely on family, friends, and nurses to bring me food. It was a nightmare.

And yet, I didn't want to be anywhere else. It wasn't easy to be there, but I knew Mark wanted me there for support and to be his voice. If the roles were reversed, he would be right by my side. I wanted to support him and be there. I wasn't going to leave his side.

At the same time, I wanted to be with Hannah. I couldn't see her and I knew she'd be confused as she still was not feeling well herself. She didn't know why Mommy wasn't tucking her in at night.

It was a woman's absolute worst nightmare. In fact, at one point, I overheard two nurses talking about how worried they were about me and how I was handling everything. I admit, I was pretty depressed and had a hard time talking to anyone. I pretty much just sat there staring at machines or trying to sleep in an uncomfortable chair (recliners weren't allowed in ICU).

Luckily, my mom knew I needed my baby girl, so she made the hour-long trip to bring her to see me every couple days. It was what I needed to get through that time.

Mark was out of it. In fact, he didn't remember any of the hospitalization when he was eventually discharged home. He had a breathing tube in for four days. He couldn't talk. He could barely follow commands. Sometimes it felt like it was pointless to be there. It was hard to be there and not hear him talk or see any movement.

The doctors and nurses kept encouraging me to talk to him. They said he may not respond visibly, but it helps him to "come to" just talking to him and holding his hand. Guess who he first responded to and squeezed the hand? Mine.

He knew I was there.

At one point, his sister-in-law called. She wanted to talk to Mark, so I put the phone up to his ear. Even though he had the breathing tube in and couldn't talk, he nodded and gave two thumbs up. He was out of it, but somehow he recognized her when he heard her voice.

When I held his hand he squeezed it hard. He didn't want to let it go. At times he rubbed my hand, as if comforting me, and making sure I was okay. He couldn't communicate much, but I knew he knew I was there.

My favorite memory was when he proved he knew I was there. Mark underwent several tests while he had the breathing tube in to see how he would do breathing on his own. During one of them, the nurse's back was to us. I reached for his hand. The nurse suddenly turned around and said, "Oh, I was wondering why he suddenly relaxed! You took his hand!" I used this proof for years after to prove that I relaxed him and didn't bring his blood pressure up like he sometimes claimed.

He knew my touch.

Whenever I told him I was right by his side and wasn't leaving, he would nod and squeeze my hand to show me he understood. He needed and wanted me there.

He knew my promise to be there.

I admit, it wasn't easy to be there--not at all. Never mind the fact that I was also sick with influenza, but to sit there all day watching your husband suffer and not respond is a horrible nightmare. I wanted to cry and scream. Most of the time I was alone, only in the company of my husband who couldn't talk and doctors and nurses whom I had never met before in my life. And I was sick with influenza. I hated it.

But I wasn't there for me. I was there for Mark, to support him, love him, and let him know I wasn't leaving his side, and I wouldn't want to be anywhere else. God gave me some special moments while Mark couldn't communicate and was unresponsive for awhile. Moments that proved Mark knew I was there and could hear my voice, feel my touch and hopefully give him some strength to keep fighting. As horrible that nightmare experience was, I'm thankful God gave me that.

After a long, gruesome couple weeks of fighting for his life and in the hospital, Mark finally made it back home. His goal was to be discharged from the hospital, get home, and dance with Hannah. He eventually got his wish. It was magic to witness their pleasure being able to dance with each other. Mark was weak and held onto the counter with his left hand as he cautiously moved his feet while Hannah's tiny hands clutched onto Mark's right hand and moved her chubby little legs as fast as they would go. She loved dancing and having her dad next to her was important to her. It was important to Mark too. She was happy to have her dancing partner back because dancing was something they loved to do together.

It was that experience that helped me realize just how important it is to live in the moment. True, Mark didn't remember the hospitalization after the fact, but he knew at the time. He knew I was there. He knew I wasn't going to leave. He knew someone he loved was there. He knew he could fight through it because he had someone who loved him so much that she would sit right there with him the whole time even when she was terribly sick at the time.

And that's why it's important to be present and be there for your loved ones, even when it is "too hard" or when it doesn't seem like it makes a difference.

--------------------◆◆◆◆◆--------------------

In December 2014, a horrific tragedy struck our small community that we live in. Kari Milberg was involved in a terrible car accident. It took the lives of Kari's daughter and her two nieces and left Kari fighting for her life with a severe traumatic brain injury.

I didn't know the family at the time, but their story touched my heart. I couldn't imagine what they were going through. A grandma losing three granddaughters with a daughter in critical condition. Each of the sisters losing a child. The heartbreak they were dealing with was too much to fathom.

I joined their memorial page on Facebook and would occasionally reach out with some encouragement, Bible verse, or something that touched my heart. I didn't think I was doing much. But when I eventually met the family, I was moved by how much they said it really did help them. It meant something because a stranger offered support.

We continued to keep in touch and our families became closer. One day I was talking with Kari's sister about Kari's traumatic brain injury. She said, "A brain injury affects everything. It's not on the surface so people do not see it as a disability. But from my experience, it's one of the worst disabilities. Each and every day is different for Kari."

I'll never forget that. I remember when she told me that, I closed my eyes and literally thanked God that with all the difficulties Mark had, he didn't have a brain injury. I just couldn't imagine that.

Unfortunately, I do now.

In April 2016, Mark was dealing with some balance issues with debilitating dizziness. Dizziness was actually a problem he had had for years. It was yet another complication from his diabetes. But it seemed to be slowly getting worse and worse.

Finally, I took him to the ER. That was when we were told that most likely Mark was suffering from nerve damage to the brain from his diabetes. Mark had lived with diabetes for over fifty years at this point, which was longer than most people who had lived with the disease. In fact, this doctor stated he had never seen a patient who had lived longer than Mark with type 1 diabetes. We were told because Mark had surpassed such expectations, he was dealing with complications they normally don't see. Unfortunately, this meant the nerve damage was going to get worse.

This was heartbreaking news to us. While this did make sense, in my heart I felt there was something else wrong. There probably was nerve damage, but I also felt we were dealing with something more.

I brought him in to see his neurologist (nerve doctor). This doctor actually thought Mark's issues were more likely due to medication side effects and not nerve damage. Mark had recently started a new medication so we were hopeful that he was right. These were encouraging words to hear! The plan was to slowly taper off this medication. The neurologist was hopeful this would help his symptoms.

But as Mark was tapering off the medication, he was having even more difficulty, twitching, balance issues, and falls. Things weren't getting better, only worse. In my heart, I felt something more was wrong. But when I asked the doctor about it again, I was told to give it time. Sometimes it takes awhile to get the medication out of the system. Hearing this, I felt satisfied that it would get better, and I didn't pursue it further. I wish I had.

I had taken a week off work in May 2016 to celebrate our fifteenth wedding anniversary. Our plan was to go on our annual vacation to the North Shore where we spent our honeymoon. However, because Mark was not feeling the best, we decided to stay at home and get a few things done. For a special treat, we planned one night in the Twin Cities at Hannah's favorite hotel. We had a wonderful night. Hannah was in her glory at the kids' pool. The smiles and joy on the faces of both Hannah and Mark were priceless. It was truly a special time for everyone. Despite Mark not feeling "right" (still feeling off balance) and needing help even to walk, this time together was precious.

Then tragedy struck.

At 4 a.m., Mark woke me up with uncontrollable shaking in his right leg. The moment I woke up, Mark asked me to call 9-1-1 which was something he rarely told me to do. I knew it was serious. Having to call 9-1-1 is scary enough. But having to call in a town you're unfamiliar with, at a hotel, in what you know is a life and death situation, was a horrible nightmare.

By the time the ambulance arrived at our hotel room, Mark couldn't even stand up on his own. He was able to talk and understand what was being said to him, but he wasn't able to follow commands. It was like his brain wasn't able to communicate with the rest of his body and tell it what to do. Two emergency personnel had to work together to lift him onto the gurney and lay him down. He was completely dead weight. They quickly got him out of the hotel and rushed him to the University of Minnesota. This was where he had had his kidney transplant fourteen years ago.

God's loving arms protected us during this time. The hotel we were staying at was about fifteen minutes away from the best hospital Mark could go to with his transplant history. If we had been at our house, we would have been an hour and a half away. If we had been at the North Shore, like our original plan, we would have been hours away. The outcome could have been much different. Being close to the University of Minnesota quite possibly changed the course of this journey.

By the time I got Hannah and myself packed up and out the door, we were about twenty minutes behind the ambulance. When we got to the ER, they had Mark stabilized, but he still couldn't talk. I noticed his right side was shaking every five minutes or so. The doctor thought the shaking was his tremors that he always had, but I knew it was different. Usually his tremors involved just his hands and on both sides of his body. These tremors involved his right side only, involved both his arm and leg, and they were not occurring all the time like his normal tremors.

Mark couldn't make a sound, but I could tell by the look in his eyes that he was terrified. He knew something was wrong.

I asked the nurse to stay with me to watch him and monitor this shaking that I noticed. She witnessed it and agreed it was more like seizure activity and not tremors. As the doctor and nurse were discussing this, his seizure activity increased to every couple minutes and the shaking became more severe.

Obviously, I didn't want Hannah to see this. I knew Mark wouldn't want her to see it either. I quickly got her out of the room as more and more nurses and doctors were coming into the room to help. The nurses and I were trying hard to keep Hannah's mind off things by giving her Popsicles and candy at six in the morning. We gave her markers and sheets to color. It didn't change what this four-year-old little girl had to witness. She was absolutely terrified, and it broke my heart.

Just minutes later, Mark's seizures became nearly constant, more pronounced, and uncontrollable. The doctor came running out to me and said, "We need to know his code status. Is he full code? If these seizures get much worse, I'm afraid we will have to intubate him to protect his airway."

My heart sank. These are situations you never want to face and here I was faced with it head-on while holding my little girl.

Fortunately, Mark and I had talked about his code status several times. I knew he wanted to live. I knew he wanted to do anything to watch his baby girl grow up. He would want the doctor to do anything to keep him alive.

"Yes", I said. "He's full code. Do whatever you need to do." I quickly signed the paperwork. Mark had to be intubated and sedated to help control the seizures and help him breathe.

Watching all this happening was like watching a movie. It didn't seem real. It was happening so fast! We were supposed to be enjoying some quality family time at the hotel. Hannah was my little fish and loved water. She had spent most of the evening swimming in the hotel's pool. I had told her she would be able to swim again in the morning before we left the hotel. That's what we should be doing. We should be watching Hannah splashing in the pool in her favorite little Dora the Explorer swimsuit, breathing in the smell of chlorine, listening to the happy screams and voices of children as they slide down the water slide. As Mark and I smiled at each other, watching Hannah, we would be discussing what we would be having for breakfast. I wasn't supposed to be in a white hospital waiting room, breathing in the smell of bleach, listening to the beeping sounds of the machines in the hospital, talking to complete strangers, and making life-changing decisions.

Mark was taken for an emergency CT scan of his head. That was when they found a subdural hematoma or bleeding on the brain.

This was a shock to everyone including the medical staff. Mark hadn't been complaining of a headache at all. Headaches are fairly common with brain bleeds. Brain bleeds usually occur after a fall or a traumatic injury to the brain. I couldn't recall a time Mark had hit his head or had a fall recently, but Hannah and I had been out of town just a month before this happened. I didn't know if he had fallen during that time. It still wasn't adding up, but at this point, we knew we had to concentrate on the fact it was found and not become preoccupied by what caused it. He needed treatment and fast! I was grateful the bleed was found, and we finally had answers to all the issues he had been having.

When the ER doctor told me about the brain bleed, I asked him, "How serious is this? Please be honest. I don't want you to sugarcoat this."

He took a deep breath. "It's serious."

I felt like I had been punched in the stomach. I knew Hannah was standing by me, but I had to ask, "What are the chances of, well, you know? I mean, Mark has two other boys. Should I be calling them in?"

The doctor sighed. "I really can't tell you what to do. I just don't know. At this point, it could go either way. I would say it's about a 50/50 chance of him surviving."

I was living a nightmare, and it was getting worse and worse.

This couldn't be happening. Not now. I kept telling myself I had to be strong. Hannah was watching me. If I broke down, she would break down. She kept looking at me with her scared, chocolate brown eyes, trying to figure out what was going to happen. She wanted answers. She didn't know what was going on. She was terrified of the unknown.

So was I.

Being strong at this point was the only choice I had, but it was all I could do to not fall apart. I wanted to go into the corner of the cold hospital and cry.

By this time, my mom had arrived at the hospital. I had called her on our way to the ER. She had gotten in the car right away and drove straight to the hospital. I was grateful to have my mom by my side. My mom has always been the one I could call and count on no matter what time it was. She was my rock. During our marriage, I had to call her many times in the middle of the night for her help. She never hesitated to be there for us. I'll always be grateful to have her wonderful support.

I asked my mom to entertain Hannah so I could make a few phone calls.

One of the first people I called was Mark's brother, Scott. He was the brother who had donated his kidney to Mark. Mark felt closest to Scott, and I knew I could count on him for prayers. I sobbed as I told him what was going on. I remember telling Scott that I was scared, and I didn't know what to do. Scott said, "I know what we're going to do. We're going to pray." Later I found out that after we hung up, he went to find his wife and just told her, "We need to pray." They got down on their knees and prayed.

I knew the hospital was no place for Hannah to be, so I called my friend, April. She came down to the hospital to pick up Hannah and took her to her house. Being separated from Hannah at that time was one of the hardest things I've ever had to do, but I knew it needed to be done. I couldn't leave Mark and yet Hannah couldn't be there either.

She knew how serious things were. As we hugged goodbye, her sad eyes filled with tears and she said, "I love you, Mommy." I told her it was okay to cry, and she sobbed into my arms. Knowing I couldn't comfort my child when she needed it most, and not knowing if she would ever see her dad alive again, was heartbreaking. Watching her walk away hand-in-hand with April was hard, even though I knew she was in excellent hands and would be well taken care of.

Mark was intubated for three days. When the tube was taken out, he was still unresponsive for days. The doctors said the longer it took for him to wake up, the less likelihood of recovery of any kind.

With each passing day, doctors cautioned me that while it was too early to tell for sure, the prognosis of a full recovery was looking more and more grim. They could not predict what, if any, function he'd get back.

I held Mark's hand and prayed to God. I pleaded if Mark wasn't able to make a full recovery, to please take him home. I knew Mark wouldn't want to live paralyzed and unable to talk or live at home. I knew Mark knew the Lord and eternity would be much better for him than his life on Earth. I cried many times, "Please Lord, fix this or take him home."

I asked all my family and friends to pray that same prayer. Many tried to encourage me and tell me that Mark would be okay and pull through. I knew people were trying to be comforting, but they hadn't witnessed all the suffering Mark had endured. I didn't want him to have to go through anymore than he already had. I truly wanted God to fix it or take him home. It may seem strange but it was most comforting to me when I asked one friend for prayers and she said, "I won't pray for God to fix this. I'm going to pray for God to take him home. Enough is enough." It was hard to hear, but it was true, and I felt understood.

God answered our prayers.

After several days, Mark slowly showed signs of waking up. At first, we were concerned because he could only move his right arm and only smile on his right side. This usually means a deep brain injury which meant he might not gain function back on his left side. When he first started speech therapy, he couldn't even open his mouth. He had to have a feeding tube inserted so he could get his medications and some nutrition into his body.

His brain wasn't able to comprehend what it needed to do to live. While it's hard to imagine sitting there watching someone you love not being able to do anything, I couldn't imagine how Mark felt having someone do literally everything for him.

Not knowing the future outcome was hard. The doctors kept telling me it was impossible to predict what Mark would gain back and what he wouldn't. Our biggest enemy was time. All we could do was wait. Wait and see what happened.

Would he ever remember who I was? Would he be able to talk again? Was he going to walk again? Would he ever be able to feed himself? He couldn't even smile. He couldn't squeeze my hand. The thought of taking care of someone who couldn't walk or feed himself was scary. Being a caregiver up to this point had been hard enough. I wasn't sure I could handle doing much more than what I already had been doing. To think of Mark not being able to do the simple things we all took for granted like walking and eating was heartbreaking and overwhelming. What if that was Mark's life now? What if he was totally dependent on me? Would he even want to live that way? I wanted a better life for him and my heart felt for him.

But we started seeing slow progress. The first time Mark smiled—delightful! The first time Mark said my name—I was captivated. The first time he squeeze my hand—I was thrilled. The first time he stuck out his tongue at me—*priceless*.

Remember at the beginning of this part of our journey, I mentioned the Milberg family? I knew while dealing with traumatic brain injury was new for me, it certainly wasn't to them. They were a rock of support for me from their encouragement, to advice on which rehab facilities to go to, and how to adjust when (or if) we did make it back to our house. God brought us together. Their support was a huge important part of our lives. They have become lifelong friends.

God will bring people into our lives to help guide us. I'm blessed He brought the Milberg family to us in our time of need. I was able to comfort them in their time of need, and they were able to comfort us in ours.

After three weeks of being in the hospital and making slow steady progress, Mark was stable enough to be moved to a rehab facility. We spent another couple weeks with speech, physical, and occupational therapy every day. As exhausting as it was for Mark, it was the step he needed to take to come home. He was willing to do anything to come home to his wife and daughter.

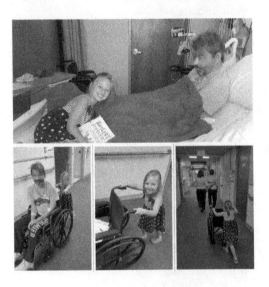

Hannah visiting Daddy at rehab

Eventually, Mark was released from the rehab facility, and we were able to come back to our house. He continued with occupational and physical therapy three times a week. Coming home was filled with hope and progress.

But it was also sad and frustrating. We were grieving the "old Mark" and learning about the "new Mark". I grieved things Mark used to say or do without knowing what would come back.

Mark ended up making an amazing recovery. In many ways, Mark had to start over. He had to learn and remember things that used to come easy for him. Over time, he was able to get most of his function back which was a miracle considering how long it took for him to respond initially. I noticed he would get frustrated and angry easier. When this happened, I simply needed to remind Mark to calm down. He would realize he was getting too upset, and he would work hard to calm himself down. Mark was usually a calm and patient person. He had a carefree attitude prior to his brain bleed. However, after his brain bleed, this wasn't the case. All things considered, we were fortunate Mark didn't have more detrimental effects from his brain bleed.

A brain injury is one of the most difficult disabilities family members endure. It is something I wouldn't wish on my worst enemy. Every day is a challenge. Every day you wake up not really knowing what to expect from your loved one.

It is possible without the rapid care Mark received, he may have had more brain damage. It is probable he may not have survived. As it was, it is truly a miracle he recovered as well as he did. God changed our anniversary plans so we were able to get the best possible medical care at just the right time. I will forever be grateful for that divine intervention.

God has always prepared us and provided for different situations.

CHAPTER 11

FEELING BLESSED AFTER SURGERY

I woke up one morning on just a normal day. I didn't expect to be on the phone scheduling Mark for an urgent surgery for the next day, but that's what happened. Every day was unpredictable during our marriage, and I had to be prepared for anything. I always had a mental plan on what I needed to do if Mark went into the hospital that day: where Hannah would go, who would take care of the dog, etc.

A month earlier, Mark had gone in for his defibrillator check. He had had a good report. No serious episodes of irregular heart rhythm, and his battery life in his defibrillator was expected to last nine years.

So when Mark started hearing odd beeping noises from his defibrillator one night, it was strange. I called the device clinic immediately the next morning. They did an at-home device check, and again, everything came back fine. However, after further investigation and review, it was discovered that Mark's particular model and brand of defibrillator had a recall and had malfunctioned. His defibrillator was no longer working. He would need to have a replacement right away.

It was discouraging. We had just been told the battery was good for nine years. Now, we had to schedule a replacement surgery for the very next day. Needless to say, we were both quite frustrated.

We asked for prayer, and the response was wonderful. We had many people praying and thinking of Mark. We were extremely grateful for such widespread support.

We woke up at the break of dawn and drove to the clinic which was more than an hour away from our house. Getting ready for surgery, Mark still wasn't himself. I could tell he was not happy about things and discouraged. I didn't blame him.

His surgery lasted an hour. The surgeon came out to tell me that everything went great, and there were no issues at all.

I went back to see Mark. I was relieved to see he looked much better. He was more relaxed, and there was color in his cheeks. The first thing he said to me was, "I'm blessed."

I gave him a funny look. "Blessed? To have surgery? What do you mean?"

He explained that recently he had started lifting weights after he did his daily walk on the treadmill. He told me he started that for a reason, to "help strengthen his muscles". He went on to say, "God helped me prepare for this surgery, and I am blessed it went so well."

Wow.

I admit on that morning that we got the call and I had to schedule an emergency surgery, I was stressed and discouraged. I also was trying to figure out things with Hannah and her schedule, getting time off of work, etc. I never thought of any of this as a "blessing". Even when Mark was out of surgery and everything went fine, I never thought of me as being "blessed"---relieved, yes, but blessed was pushing it.

That is, until Mark said he was blessed. He had just undergone a surgery that was completely unpredictable. While the surgery itself was relatively low risk, there were still concerns because of Mark's low heart function. There are people who don't walk away from minor surgeries, but he did.

Yes, he was blessed. We were blessed.

When we parked at the hospital, Mark couldn't get out of the car for several minutes because a woman was getting a child in a wheelchair out of a car. Not being able to open a door and being a little late to an appointment was minor compared to this child and woman's lifestyle. Mark could walk. This child wasn't able to.

Yes, he was blessed.

Just a week before Mark's surgery, we had heard of an acquaintance who had had a heart attack, had bypass surgery, and was fighting for his life. Mark was able to have a surgery in the hospital, leave that same day, and go to sleep in his own bed.

Yes, he was blessed.

Mark was right. It was strange to walk in and see him covered in sterile gauze, sterile solution, an IV poking out of him, gauze all over his arm from blood draws, and hear him say, "I'm blessed". But it was true. He was blessed. We were blessed.

Mark said God helped him through it. He helped him prepare for the surgery, and it was all in God's timing.

What a blessing.

CHAPTER 12

LIFE AS A CAREGIVER

I'm sure many people have heard of survivor's guilt. It is guilt someone feels when they survive a traumatic event when others don't. While I didn't have survivor's guilt per se, it's the best description of how I struggled for a long time while married to Mark.

It was our joke that Mark had more lives than a cat. The reason he lived as long as he did was simply a miracle. It can't be explained any other way. Whenever Mark had a setback, we always knew he would bounce back. I heard all the time, "Don't worry, this is Mark. He'll pull through this", and he always did. It truly was a miracle. Even when we were told he only had hours to live, many people were saying, "This is Mark. He'll be fine." Throughout our marriage I always wondered why he was the one to pull through and others didn't. Mark had more than "nine lives". He always pulled through but so many others passed away suddenly. It seemed as though others could contribute more to the community or do much more for other people than Mark could.

My conflicting emotions about Mark's survival when other healthy fathers died is best described as "survivor's guilt". It was a guilt I felt every day. Why did I feel guilty that my husband lived when other wives lost theirs? It was hard for me to understand. It was confusing to feel grateful to God and yet struggle greatly to understand.

A car accident takes the life of three beautiful young girls who had their whole lives ahead of them. Why them? Our small community suddenly and unexpectedly loses a wonderful wrestling coach and mentor for many kids, and a family is left mourning a wonderful man. Then, the same thing happened again a short time later. Why?

We heard many times that Mark defied the odds. He was lucky. Other people with his struggles didn't survive nearly as long as he did.

Why was that? It didn't seem fair.

I know the simple answer: "God wasn't finished with him yet." Mark was fulfilling his purpose on Earth. I get that. I understand, and I know it. I am sure it will all make sense when I see Jesus face-to-face, and He clarifies why, or at that moment it won't matter anymore.

But I admit it was hard when I saw Mark struggle every day. Mark had constant pain. Some days were better than others. Some days he was in so much pain he was screaming, crying, lying on the floor, and clutching his feet. Sometimes he clutched his feet so hard the skin on his feet broke open and bled. He was desperate to lessen the pain. He felt if he could open up his skin the pain would come out. I can't imagine living with that kind of pain, and he had to do it for years.

There was one day in 2002 when I prayed to God to give Mark one day where he would wake up and tell me, "Wow! I feel good! Let's do this, let's do that!", and at the end of the day, I would feel exhausted from doing so much because he finally had one good day with no pain.

I'm happy to report that God, in fact, did answer my prayer. One day early in our marriage, to the surprise of many, Mark woke up with no pain. We went shopping, had a picnic, and hiked. At the end of the day, I was exhausted---but Mark wasn't. It was the best day of our married life. A true answer to prayer. It was the only day he didn't have pain.

I saw his pain, fatigue, sickness, and discouragement every day. I saw the fight and determination in his eyes, but every day was a struggle. I knew he would spend eternity in Heaven with no pain, so seeing him struggle here wasn't easy. I didn't struggle with a lot of anger after Mark passed away, but I did struggle with anger when Mark was here. I prayed to God to heal Mark or take him home. His suffering was too much for all of us to bear.

We were married almost nineteen years. In our marriage vows, we promised "till death do us part, in sickness and in health". Mark was very sick when we got married. When we were saying our vows and I said to Mark "in sickness and in health", I squeezed his hands and choked out the words with tears pooling in my eyes.

I took them seriously.

I knew I would never leave him, but I'd be lying if I said I never thought about it. Because, let me repeat, when I said my vows I took them seriously. I knew I would never, ever leave Mark. We went through a lot in the 18-1/2 years of our marriage. We struggled a lot. I believe we were tested many times. We hit rock bottom. And yet, we made it through.

I heard a story about a wife caring for her husband who had cancer. She was tired of caring for him, and she beat him to death. She is now serving life in prison. One reporter was quoted as saying, "All she had to do was wait a few months, and he would have died from the cancer. I don't know what she was thinking." I do. You hit rock bottom. You're exhausted. You're scared. You don't know what to do anymore, especially if you aren't getting help. I understand why she did what she did. My heart hurts for her, while also, feeling sorry that her husband suffered a more terrible death at the hands of someone he likely thought would never hurt him.

I also heard of a man who committed suicide after taking care of his wife for two years with a traumatic brain injury. He had hit rock bottom. He couldn't cope with his wife's needs without help. Some thought he was selfish. I thought he was overwhelmed. My heart broke for him and his wife.

I understand that "rock bottom" feeling. While the whole world judged these people, I am among the minority who understood and felt compassion for them. Even though I would never take the action they did, I understand how it feels when you just can't handle your circumstances anymore. At that point, even the smallest things, like brushing your teeth, are too hard. I know what it's like to take a shower just so you can have a good cry without anyone else knowing. I know what it's like to feel completely alone even when the phone is ringing off the hook and texts are pouring in. I know what it's like to punch a wall because you're faced with the most difficult decision of whether or not to put your spouse in a nursing home, and you are scared to make a decision.

Yes, I had fleeting thoughts of leaving Mark, of what my life would be like if I hadn't married him. It was hard. It was trying. I yelled at Mark. I cried many tears in sadness, frustration, guilt, you name it. I've hit rock bottom, but somehow I've managed to claw my way back. It's not because I always wanted to be a caregiver to Mark. It's not because I couldn't have a better life. It's because I'm not living my life for me. I'm living it for God.

I admit things were far from easy. Many times I felt like throwing in the towel. Still, there was a side of me that no matter how hard it got, I wouldn't give up. I loved Mark, and I love how God works. Did I wish things were easier? Yes. Did I get down about it? More than anyone knows.

But the truth is, I can't imagine life any other way. When I hear about the stories like the ones above, I understand. I get it. I can be their voice. Maybe that's part of what I'm supposed to do. Maybe that's part of what God's purpose is for my life. Show and tell others what it's like.

Life is hard. If you find yourself with nothing left to give, remember God makes sure there is always someone who has been there and someone who gets it. They are the ones to help you find a way back up.

Life is worth it. There are hard times. Just don't forget there are also good times.

————— ✦✦✦✦✦✦ —————

When Mark and I got married, we knew life would be hard for us. What we didn't do was stop living. If anything, we lived more. Just because Mark struggled with health issues, we weren't going to just sit around and let me take care of him.

My uncle gave us the best advice at our wedding: Dream Big. And dream big we did.

A year after Mark's transplant we bought a house together. We had been renting a house right across the street from the hospital as it was much easier to live across the street for appointments and the endless ER trips with Mark's condition. We were in the ER so much that when I called they knew my voice. It was a blessing we were able to live in that house. God provided for us.

But it was our dream to purchase our own house. One year after his transplant surgery when Mark was feeling a little better, we started looking at houses. We found one we both loved and purchased it. It was just a few blocks from the hospital!

We also dreamed of having a baby, and we did everything to make that happen. Our circumstances weren't ideal to raise a child but the truth is no one knows if they will get cancer, injured, or when our time is finished. Does that mean we need to stop dreaming and stop living? Nope. If anything we need to live more fervently. We need to say yes. Take a chance. Live freely. Life is a precious gift that we can't take for granted and assume it will always be here.

I can't put into words how much Hannah meant to Mark and how much she changed his life. The seven years that Mark was blessed to be a father to her, he had smiled and laughed more than I had seen in all the years we had been together.

We lived an amazing, dream-fulfilled life.

We were also realistic. Mark and I had some hard conversations.

Conversations with lots of tears and hugs. Conversations most people never have or think about having. I have no regrets. We always said what we needed to say and prepared for any eventuality. I'm not saying it wasn't easy when it was time to say goodbye to Mark. In fact, it was the most difficult thing I've ever had to do. But I was at peace knowing we had prepared as well as we could have.

We cherished every single day. We lived for today, not tomorrow. We never thought, "That can wait." We thought, "This can't wait. Let's do it now." Because we never know when doing it now won't be an option.

For example, since I was a little girl, I dreamed of ice skating at the Rockefeller Center at Christmastime. It was on my bucket list. When Hannah arrived, my dream expanded to skating there with my daughter. I started talking to Mark about it in September 2015. I was making some plans but then "life" happened. The dishwasher broke down. Then, there was another unexpected expense followed by this problem and that stress. I told Mark we would plan it for the following year. I'll never forget feeling his hand on my shoulder and turning around to see the serious look on his face. "Tammy, do it. Do it this year. Don't wait. I want to see you guys do this before it's too late." I knew what he was saying. At that moment, I nodded. I knew I needed to make this happen, not just for myself, but for Mark.

So I made the reservations. I fulfilled my dream with my daughter by my side and my husband watching with the biggest smile on his face that I had ever seen. Living my dream was living his dream. I'm glad he convinced me to make that trip. He ended up struggling with severe pain at the end of the trip. The flight home was extremely rough. It was the last time he ever flew on an airplane. I'm glad that on his last trip, he was able to see something that made all of us happy.

Yes, we struggled. But, we dreamed big. And, we lived.

Tomorrow is not promised. Our days are numbered. Dream big. Live big. Don't live like you're dying. Live like you're living.

And give your spouses and children hugs and kisses. Tell them you love them every single day. You won't regret it.

CHAPTER 13

Enrolling In Hospice

In 2016, one of my friends casually mentioned we should look into hospice to help with Mark's pain. Mark and I both immediately shut that idea down. In fact, to be honest, we were a bit offended it was even suggested. In our minds, hospice meant "end of life", death, and "giving up". Mark wasn't ready to die by any means. He was desperate to live and see his daughter grow up. Looking back, I realize how little we knew how hospice services work these days.

We didn't even think about hospice for a couple years. Then, my friend, Monique Schaffer, who works for St. Croix Hospice, would occasionally post on Facebook about how hospice wasn't just "end-of-life" cares. It was also a way for chronically ill patients to improve the quality of their remaining life. After seeing several of her posts, I reached out to her to get more information. She was encouraging and patient with me as I continued to reach out over and over, asking questions, and yet not wanting to really commit to talking too much about it. After all, it was emotional just talking about hospice. The thought of enrolling into hospice was scary. It was a tough and emotional step to make.

She never pressured. She only offered kindness and understanding. You could tell Monique loved what she did. She sincerely wanted what was best for people and wanted to help.

Mark's nerve pain got to the point where he couldn't take it anymore. I'm honestly surprised he was able to hold out for as long as he did. I don't think I could have done it if I were in his shoes. He was the strongest man I knew.

The thought of getting some comfort and improving his quality of life gave him hope of relief that he hadn't felt in a long time. But he didn't want to be seen as "end of life" or "giving up". We met with Monique and a nurse from St. Croix Hospice. Mark had a few things that were important to him if he were to enroll in hospice: 1. He wanted all his medical care and decisions to be discussed with his primary doctor whom had cared for him for twenty years. Mark trusted him and wanted him involved with his care. 2. He wanted to stay on all of his medications. 3. He wanted to be full code which meant if he needed CPR or life-saving treatment, he wanted it to be done as he wasn't ready to die.

St. Croix Hospice was more than happy to work with Mark on these things. There is a misconception about hospice that you have to stop medications, have your code status be DNR (no resuscitation efforts if needed and no life-saving efforts), and you couldn't have your primary physician involved in your care anymore. But we found out those things weren't true. When we met with St. Croix Hospice, the nurse told Mark, "This is your journey and we want to make this what you are most comfortable with, Mark. We are here for you."

After meeting with St. Croix Hospice in February 2019, Mark enrolled himself into the hospice program. His goal was to get better control of his pain and have a better quality of life. He wanted to do more things with Hannah. He wanted to enjoy his remaining time with her. St. Croix Hospice was determined to do what they could to achieve this. St. Croix Hospice also was sensitive to the fact that Hannah was only seven years old and would have questions about why nurses were coming to the house. They asked how we wanted them to answer her questions and explain situations to Hannah if needed. For parents who were worried about how their daughter would handle things, their support and concern meant a lot to us.

That wasn't the only reason Mark decided to enroll into the hospice program. He also knew it would take pressure off me as a caregiver. Hospice is one of few programs that aren't just there to provide care for the patient, but also for the caregivers. Hospice would pay for a nurse and a nurse's aide to come to our house twice a week or more if needed. I didn't have to schedule any doctor's appointments. I didn't have to worry about Mark's medications, getting them set up, or getting refills. The nurse would check on Mark, take his vital signs, and call the doctor if anything needed attention. The aide would help Mark with self-cares including showers and shaving, etc.

I could be Mark's wife again. For years, I felt more like a nurse, a pharmacist, and a chauffeur to appointments. It wasn't Mark's fault by any means. It was the reality of life when you were married to a chronically ill spouse. For eighteen years, I was his primary caregiver. I watched his every move, helped him with self-cares, made appointments, and called doctors. I was stressed and exhausted all the time.

But when Mark was enrolled in hospice, I was able to sit and watch a movie with him. I was able to relax, smile, and enjoy his company. I was his wife. Instead of his caregiver, I was his support system that he needed physically and emotionally. I could give 100 percent to him. Mark could see the difference in me. He was glad he enrolled in hospice and took that pressure off me. That was his way of taking care of me and his family.

Another deciding factor in enrolling into the hospice program was that St. Croix Hospice would continue to support Hannah and I with any counseling or bereavement needs up to thirteen months after Mark's death. To Mark, that was the most important and really the final deciding factor. Mark was always worrying about Hannah and me and how we would be taken care of after he had passed. He made sure the house maintenance was taken care of so I wouldn't have to worry about the house in the future. He wanted to do everything he could to make sure we would be okay. Knowing that we would have the emotional support we needed after he passed was extremely important to him.

Even so, it wasn't easy being enrolled in hospice. To be approved, Mark was required to have a life expectancy of six months or less. While being approved was a relief to us, it was also a reality check. Mark was expected to live less than six months. This didn't mean it was definite as people have been enrolled in hospice for years with the same life expectancy. We also knew only God truly knew Mark's life expectancy. But this was still an emotional reality we were dealt with.

While having the nurses and aides coming in quite often was extremely helpful, most of the discussions revolved around helping Mark with his pain and keeping him comfortable, not necessarily upcoming surgeries or procedures to prolong his life. The hope we felt was simply Mark getting comfort, not life-saving measures. At times, those were hard discussions to have as the reality would sink in as to the reason Mark was enrolled in hospice. Watching Mark struggle to get dressed and needing help with simple self-cares like shaving and taking a shower was difficult for me.

For the nine months that Mark was enrolled in hospice, we not only gained some much needed help, support, pain relief, and comfort for Mark, we also gained a second family. We saw his nurse and nurse's aide more than our own family. The care and love they showed our family was amazing.

There was one day Mark was really bothered by something. The nurse knew something was wrong, but Mark kept insisting he was fine. She finally got Mark to open up about what was bothering him. She stayed for two hours talking with him. She didn't leave until Mark was feeling better. That meant a lot to both him and me. It showed how much they care for their patients.

Hospice was a saving grace and proved to be invaluable for our family. We didn't realize how important hospice would be until we were preparing to take a family vacation to Hawaii. God had orchestrated interventions in our lives once again.

CHAPTER 14

MARK'S JOURNEY TO HIS HEAVENLY HOME

Usually when you're planning a dream family trip to Hawaii, you don't have a bad feeling about it.

But I did.

In Christmas 2018, my parents gifted my siblings, me, and all the grandchildren a trip to Hawaii. We had originally planned to go in the spring 2019, but the only opening for their timeshare was the third week of September 2019. It wasn't ideal. The kids would be starting school the day after Labor Day and would be in school just over a week before taking a week off for a family vacation. That was just when they would be getting back into the swing of things at school. It certainly was not what we wanted, but it was what was available. So we made our travel plans.

As September approached, I was still nervous about taking Hannah out of school. I was feeling guilty about taking "Hannah-time" away from Mark. I was also feeling anxious about leaving Mark. Just a few weeks before we were to be leaving, he had been in the hospital suffering from shingles in his right eye. The thought of leaving him when he was still recovering from that horrible experience was torturing me.

I told him I had a really bad feeling about going, and I was seriously considering staying home. He looked at me with a serious expression, and somewhat angry tone of voice, and said, "Absolutely not. You're going. If you don't want to go for yourself, go for Hannah."

Whoa. Okay then. It was decided I was going no matter what.

I wanted to respect Mark's wishes. I knew taking care of his family was his first priority. He didn't want us to miss out on opportunities because of his needs. Respecting his wishes and his dreams was my way of supporting and providing for him. At this point in his life, I allowed him to make his own decisions about his healthcare. If a Big Mac was what sounded good to him, I would get him a Big Mac. He was often nauseous and vomiting. If he was able to eat something and keep it down, that was a success. If he wasn't interested in having the hospice nurse come in one day and would rather rest, I would cancel his appointments. I allowed him to make his own decisions and live his life the way he wanted to.

This also meant if he said I was going to Hawaii, I respected him. I told him I would go if he wanted me to, even if I was hesitant. If it was important to him, it was important to me.

It wasn't easy arranging it though. Mark basically needed round-the-clock care. Since he was enrolled in the hospice program, we had the benefit of having "caregiver relief". This was a benefit in which he could be admitted into a nursing home for five days. Mark was not happy at all about doing that, but we didn't really have other options. Even with those five days, there were still four days that he would be at home and needed care. He needed his medications monitored, pain patches and medication applied to his feet, help with giving his insulin shots, and getting meals. There was a lot to think about. My main support system who came through in these types of situations was my family, but they were going to be in Hawaii with me. It was a real struggle trying to come up with a schedule to make sure he was covered.

It took a lot of calls and planning with tears and elevated stress, but I was finally able to come up with a plan. I knew Mark would be well taken care of.

Little did I know that schedule would be thrown out the window after a couple days.

I explained everything to Mark and went through the schedule with him. As I was going through it, again I told him I had a really bad feeling. Of course he told me not to worry and everything would be okay. But I just couldn't shake it.

"Okay Mark, hear me out. What if something happens? What if you get really sick? I'll be far away."

In typical Mark fashion, he simply said, "Nothing will happen."

"But Mark, what if it does? I hate to think about it, but what if you are dying?"

Mark calmly said, "Everything will be ready for you to take care of when you come back."

"But do you want me to come back?"

Mark shook his head. "No. I want you to stay. Stay and have a good time. I'll be okay."

I started to cry. "I don't know Mark. I don't know if I could stay. I really don't think I could. I would want to be there for you."

"I want you to stay. Stay for Hannah."

I sighed. "Okay, I would stay. But I promise I would make sure you wouldn't be alone. Who would you want to be there if I couldn't?"

He thought for a second and then mentioned our close friends.

"Okay, Mark. I would make sure they are there. I promise. Okay now that we have that taken care of, I feel better. Now we don't have to talk about that again." We both smiled and talked about something else.

Little did I know just how vital and critical that conversation was.

The morning we left, it wasn't easy for me to leave him. The thought of leaving him for over a week and being far away was hard. When I got the text from my mom saying they were just a few minutes away to pick us up, I started crying. I sat by Mark as he held me. He comforted me the best he could, but I could tell he was sad too. Hannah ran to another room as seeing me cry was hard on her.

She had a hard time saying goodbye to Mark, but I made her give him a hug. That is something that haunts me to this day. Her last hug with her dad was "forced". If I hadn't given into my emotions, Hannah would have remained in her positive and upbeat mood. She would have been excited about Hawaii and not reminded about being away from her dad.

My parents' van pulled into the driveway. They grabbed our suitcases to put into the van. I gave Mark a hug and kiss goodbye. I tried hard to control my emotions. Mark whispered to me, "I'll see you soon. It's just a week. Have fun!" I got into the van and watched as Mark stood on the deck, smiling, and waving to us. I had a strong urge to get out of the van and run to him to give him a hug. But I knew we were in a hurry to get down to the airport, so I stayed in the van and waved to him, blowing him kisses.

I wish I had gotten out of the van to get one last hug.

Driving out of the driveway and watching Mark as we drove off was hard on both Hannah and me. I held Hannah as she cried. I reminded her that we would see him soon. My friend, April, was staying with Mark for the majority of the four days he was at home. She came to the house shortly after we left, and we FaceTimed with Mark and her. Hannah gave Mark a huge smile, and she told him "I love you Dad!". Those words were the last words Hannah ever spoke to her dad. Those were cherished words that Mark told April he thought he would never hear again. Hannah was a typical seven-year-old at that time. She was much more interested in playing with her friends than spending time with boring Mom and Dad. At that point in her life, I think Mark felt left out and forgotten. Hearing her say those words were really important to him. I was glad he was able to hear them at that time.

*My friend April and Mark. This was the last
picture of Mark and his beautiful smile*

The flight to Hawaii was long but uneventful. I called Mark and April when we landed. Everything was going well. I was pleased and relieved.

On our first day in Hawaii, we decided to check out the Pololu Valley Lookout. This is a beautiful area on the Big Island in Hawaii. At the top of the lookout, the scenery is beautiful. There is a trail three quarters of a mile down the cliff to the bottom where the black sand beach meets the valley floor. This trail is steep and rocky. It is a real challenge to walk.

On the day we decided to hike this trail, it was very hot. It's always hot in Hawaii, but it was especially hot this day. We had water in the car, but we left it there so we would have it when we got back from the hike. That was a bad decision. At the last second, I decided to take a bottle of water for Hannah and me. I was glad I did.

This trail was challenging for even experienced hikers. If you weren't experienced, it was really tough. There were slippery rocks along the entire steep trail. The breathtaking views were worth the walk though. We all struggled getting down, but my dad was really struggling. He had to stop a few times on the way down to rest. I asked him multiple times if he wanted to wait and catch up with us when we came back up, but he kept insisting on continuing. He said he would rest when we got down to the bottom.

The black sand beach at the bottom was absolutely beautiful. It was definitely worth the walk down. But it was really hot. I was glad I had taken the water at the last minute. I offered some to other members of the family, but they wouldn't take any because of germs. We are a family of notable germaphobics.

The black sand beach. You can see the top of the cliff and how steep it is to the bottom

After we had rested for quite awhile at the beautiful beach, we started the difficult trek back up the cliff. Mom and Dad kept to the back as climbing up the cliff was slow. The kids were in better shape than all of us and wanted to go ahead. I chose to stay with the kids, or do my best to stay with them, while the rest of my siblings walked up with our parents.

It was an incredibly hard walk going up. It was much steeper than any of us expected. By the time the kids and I got to the top, we were exhausted. We searched for the nearest shade and plopped down. The keys to the car were with the other group, so we couldn't get any water. The only thing we could do was wait.

And wait.

And wait some more.

We were all starting to worry because it was taking such a long time. Then we saw my brother, Aaron, running up the hill. He couldn't talk too much. He was out of breath and completely exhausted. He briefly said, "Dad's in trouble" as he headed to get the car.

Dad had gotten overheated. He had gotten so dehydrated that he couldn't function. Angels surrounded my dad that day. An Emergency Room physician and his family were hiking that trail at the same time. He knew what needed to be done to help my dad. Other hikers shared their T-shirts and water. They literally dragged my dad up the cliff. Dad couldn't see anyone, but he could hear their encouraging words. He heard one person's name was Margaret, which was his mother's name who had passed away years ago. Dad could only see white. When he heard the name "Margaret", he thought to himself, "Mom is coming to take me home." He was preparing himself for his heavenly reunion with his mother.

At the top of the cliff on the lookout, the kids and I watched as the car drove up with our family in it. Dad didn't look good. He was completely pale and obviously dehydrated. We debated bringing him to the nearest hospital. He had had a severe leg injury a year before. Ever since that injury, his body was susceptible to illness and collapse. His dehydration was scary for us. Thankfully, after sitting in the air-conditioned car and drinking fluids, he started feeling better. The color started coming to his face again, and he was able to talk.

It was a sobering day for all of us. It was hard to be in a strange place, not knowing where the hospital was and dealing with a life-threatening situation. We breathed a sigh of relief when Dad was feeling back to himself. We thought the worst part of the trip was over. It was only going to get better from there. It was a scary moment for our family, but we made it through. We learned a valuable lesson to always bring water and make sure we are well-hydrated. Whew.

We put that experience behind us and focused on enjoying the rest of the trip (with plenty of water!). The nightmare was over, we thought.

But it was only beginning.

--------------------◆◆◆◆◆◆--------------------

The next day I got a call from April. She was in a panic because she couldn't find Mark's pain medications. He was in terrible pain. I could hear him screaming in the background. This was nothing new to me. I had heard him screaming in pain for years. The difference was this time he was screaming in front of other people. Nobody ever saw him scream in pain because he bit his tongue. He refused to let others see it. It was only in front of me that he didn't hold back. So hearing him scream in front of other people, I knew it was bad. Really bad.

As days went on, his pain never got better. Medications weren't helping at all. I was in constant contact with April because I knew his pain was out of control. He was screaming and crying. He was even snippy to April which was completely unheard of for him.

He was in constant and horrible pain. Finally, the day came that he was scheduled to go to the nursing home. He was still crying and screaming in pain. He was in rough shape. He couldn't walk, stand, or lift himself up. He wasn't able to shift himself in the couch or chair. He needed someone to help him even with normal functions. It was like his body was completely shutting down.

Everyone was commenting about how much pain he was in and his constant crying and screaming. In my heart, I knew this had to be the worst pain he had ever been in. Even the morphine they were giving him wasn't relieving the pain. Mark had always refused morphine because he was worried how it would affect him. I knew he was desperate when he had agreed to receiving morphine. Usually when the pain got really bad, his body would eventually get exhausted from screaming and not sleeping that he would sleep out of pure exhaustion. That wasn't even happening. I was terrified this was the end. I had never seen him in this much pain.

I texted April and voiced my thoughts. She reassured me that if it was the end, she would be by his side reminding Mark of our love for him. We also knew this was Mark. His nickname was the Energizer Bunny because he "kept going and going". It was never the end.

Seeing Mark in this much pain was a shock to friends and family as well as to the medical providers. They emphatically said he shouldn't go back home and were concerned about exposing Hannah to his intense pain. Even though I wasn't ready to give up on my promise to care for Mark at home, the time had come for me to make sure he was in a place where he could get constant supervision and pain control. I was slowly starting to realize it was impossible for one person to manage him at home.

I was in Hawaii, thousands of miles away, and feeling like I had the weight of the world on my shoulders. One thing Mark adamantly argued against was being admitted into a nursing home. It was the only request Mark made of me. He begged me not to put him in a nursing home. I knew if that ever happened he would give up and die.

It was a difficult decision I would have to make when we got home. How could I put Mark into a nursing home when I knew he desperately did not want to go? But did I really want to put Hannah through intense trauma having her see her dad suffer greatly every day? We knew it was incredibly hard on her. I had no idea what to do, and I was struggling. I was so distraught. I could only give that concern to God. There was nothing else to do.

Little did I know, that was a decision I would never have to make.

The day that all this discussion was going on, our family was at the Pearl Harbor National Memorial. Unfortunately, no phones were allowed in certain areas to show respect for people who had lost their lives. I understood, but it was hard not to be in constant contact.

While we were there, we watched a movie about the Pearl Harbor attacks. It showed the bombing and people dying which seemed to hit Hannah hard. She was screaming and crying. She asked to go back home to Daddy. I hadn't mentioned anything to Hannah about what was going on. I wonder if she had some sort of premonition that something bad was going on. I hadn't seen her that upset before.

The next morning I got the call that stopped me cold.

I was washing the dishes when April called. She hesitated. I could tell she was trying to find the right words. Then she sighed.

"Tammy, I don't think Mark is doing good at all."

I felt a sheer panic inside me. I dropped the glass I was washing into the sink. I ran into the other room with the phone. I didn't want the rest of the family to see me crying, and I wanted some privacy.

April gave me details that were hard to hear. Mark wasn't responding. They didn't know if it was because of the medications in his body or because he was dying. I knew Mark usually had a tough time waking up from any kind of sedation. I thought maybe since this was the first time he had had morphine, this could be his body reacting to the morphine. At least that was my original thought. However, when I voiced that, I was told they had tried to stop the morphine in hopes that he would become more responsive, but he wasn't. They were doubtful it was from sedation. I had a sick feeling in my stomach.

I knew what was happening. My husband was dying.

Hannah had seen me run into the room with the phone. She didn't think too much about it at first, but after I had been gone for awhile she came to look for me. I couldn't tell her what was going on, but she could see the tears in my eyes. She asked me if everything was okay. I just shook my head no.

She ran out of the room, and I hung up the phone. I walked out to the living room where I saw Hannah in tears and her cousin hugging her. The family was quiet and looking at me. They knew something bad was going on.

I started crying, "It doesn't look good. He isn't doing good at all. We need to pray, and we need to pray now."

My family all stood up and got into a circle to pray. I heard the door slam, and I knew Hannah ran out of the timeshare. Whenever she gets upset, she tends to run away and wants to be by herself. But this time there was no way I was going to let her be alone. She had no idea what was going on. She just knew that I had told everyone that Mark wasn't good. To her, this was her daddy. She was scared about what was happening.

I opened up the door and saw my baby girl sitting on the grass with tears streaming down her face. With tears of my own blurring my vision, I said a quick prayer. "God, give me the words. I don't know how to do this." How would I tell my baby girl that her dad was dying?

I tried to walk closer to Hannah. but she screamed, put her hands over her ears, and ran farther away. I knew I couldn't push it. I knew she would need the space, but I also knew she needed me. She ran to the other side of the fence that was by our car. I walked slowly up to her by the fence and bent down to her. I put my hand through the fence and on her shoulder. I didn't want to have the fence between us, but I also knew that was what she wanted and needed.

I took a deep breath—the deepest breath I had taken in my life. I said the words to my daughter that no one ever wants to say.

"Hannah, Daddy will probably be going to Heaven soon." As Hannah cried harder, I said, "I know this is so sad sweetie. We have to remember that Daddy will be with Jesus. You know how he is in so much pain all the time?" Hannah nodded. "He won't be in pain anymore, and he deserves that, doesn't he? And remember we will see him in Heaven. He gets to see Jesus! We have to concentrate on the fact that he will no longer be in pain, and he gets to be with Jesus."

As I was saying these words to Hannah, my brother, Chad, and his daughter, Adelaide, had come out. They were by Hannah's side comforting her. After more tears and a time of silence, I asked Hannah what we could do to be there for her.

"I want to play Crazy Eights with Chad and Adelaide."

So I went in the house and grabbed the cards. If that's what she wanted to do, we were going to do it. We played Crazy Eights in the driveway of the timeshare. I'm sure it looked strange to other people, but I didn't care. It was what Hannah wanted and needed. After a round of Crazy Eights, she looked at me and said, "Mom, is he listening to the Beatles? We have to make sure the Beatles are on. It's his favorite."

I smiled through my tears. "I don't know, Hannah, but I will make sure."

I found out later from April that after we had talked and hung up the phone, the nurses taking care of Mark were sobbing. They knew what was going on, and they were heartbroken. They said they usually can remain professional, but they were so moved by what was going on that they couldn't stop crying. This was affecting many people.

We decided as a family to make the day a "Hannah day". We were going to do what she wanted to do. We had plans that could easily be changed. She decided she wanted to go swimming at the resort's pool, and that was what we did. My whole family was incredibly supportive and flexible. I was grateful for that. They were all there for Hannah, helping her through this, and I was relieved for their support.

During the day, I was in constant contact with the nurses, April, and my aunt and uncle who were also with Mark. They were letting me know of any changes that were going on, but there was very little change. He still wasn't responding like he should be.

Later that afternoon Hannah requested to go to the beach. I would check my phone every couple minutes, and in between that time, I would be out in the ocean with my family. We all knew Hannah was in her element. Seeing her smile and watching my family help her smile and be there for her was such a comfort to me. I knew my family was hurting and was devastated by what was going on, but they were putting their feelings aside to help Hannah and be there for her. I couldn't be more grateful.

At one point we all decided to go out and "catch some waves".

Hannah started screaming for me to stay back on the beach. She was adamant that I not go out with everyone. I didn't understand why until she told me, "Mom, I can't lose you too."

Ouch.

I realized just how scared Hannah was. She knew she was going to lose her daddy, and she was terrified that something was going to happen to her mom too. It was at that moment that I knew I was going to do whatever I could to try to prevent that from happening.

I checked my phone again. There was nothing. I decided to go sit on the beach, watch everyone catching waves and watch Hannah play on the beach. I needed a breather. I needed to listen to the water, put my toes in the sand, let the sand slide through my fingers and just forget about everything for a little bit. I closed my eyes and took a couple deep breaths.

After about twenty minutes, I decided I should check my phone. Twenty minutes may not seem like a long time but when you know your husband could die at any time, twenty minutes is a lifetime. When I checked my phone, I saw I had two missed calls from April and a text message from her. My heart sank. As I read the text, I started sobbing.

"The hospice nurse was here and she says the end of his journey is near. Please pray for him to be welcomed by all your babies. I already told him that he was on babysitting duty for all the babies. We are keeping him comfortable and calm. We are not giving him morphine because his respirations are too low and erratic. So he was given Haldol. He doesn't seem to be in any pain. Hospice nurse does not think he will be here in the morning. She thought maybe in the next three to five hours. We are all holding him close and reminding him of yours and Hannah's love for him. His rock music is playing softly in the background. He is in good hands. We will keep this space sacred and honor his passing."

As I was reading the text, all I could hear were the waves in the ocean. Suddenly, they seemed much louder, and I wanted them to stop.

While I was sobbing, I started dialing April. The sound of the waves was deafening. I started running to the grass and away from the shoreline to get away from them but running in the sand was hard. It's even harder when you're trying desperately to get to the other side. You don't realize how difficult it is.

I finally got to the grass, and I got through to April. I could barely hear April talking as the sound of the waves was loud to me. To this day, it is hard for me to hear any kind of waves.

I started screaming and sobbing loudly. I think reality finally hit me. Mark was dying.

April told me I needed to calm down. Mark couldn't hear my anxiety, or it would make things worse. He needed to hear me calm. After a few deep breaths, my heart was still pounding. The sound of the waves was still loud. It was hard to hear, but I became calm and strong. I could say my final words to Mark. April put the phone next to his ear so he could hear my voice one last time:

"I love you Mark. I love you so much. You have been the best husband and dad we could ever ask for. I promise you we will be okay. You don't have to worry about us. We will be taken care of. I'm going to miss you so much but I know we will see each other again. I love you honey."

It wasn't the goodbye I wanted, but it would have to do.

I looked at the waves as I talked. I stood there, shaking, knowing there was nothing more I could do for Mark. I couldn't change this. I couldn't stop it any more than I could stop the aqua blue waves from coming into shore. Jesus was calling Mark, insistent as the ocean, pulling him towards home.

I could hear Hannah yelling for me. I turned and watched as she ran awkwardly across the sand with a look of terror on her face. When she caught up to me, she asked, "Did he die? Did he die?" She saw I was on the phone and sobbing. I was trying to find the words through my sobs. She knew no matter what it wasn't good news, and she ran back to the rest of the family in tears.

I told April I had to go. I hung up the phone and ran clumsily across the sand with the deafening sound of waves in the background. Usually sand and waves are a wonderful, calming effect, but at this time it was the opposite. Why did those waves have to be so loud and the sand difficult to run in?

Hannah had gotten back to my family. They saw that she was in tears and all looked to me to see what was going on.

I could barely get the words out. "He didn't die, but he only has hours left to live."

The waves were too loud. I just wanted them to stop.

It was about 5:30 p.m. in Hawaii which meant it was about 10:30 p.m. back in Wisconsin. I knew I needed to call Mark's boys. I hated that it was really late, but I also knew they needed to know. They knew their dad was not doing well. I had kept them informed with everything that was going on. The news didn't come as a surprise to them, but those were still hard phone calls to make.

Mark's youngest son, Peter, lived in the area so he immediately went to the nursing home to be by his father's side. The next day was his birthday. It was a hard reality that Mark may pass away on his son's birthday.

Mark's oldest son, Chad, lived in Colorado and wasn't able to be by his dad's side. He was able to call and say some final words. After talking to his dad for the last time, he asked if someone could pray. Everyone in that room joined together, held hands, and April said, what I was told, the most beautiful prayer. That is a beautiful scene I wish I could have seen in person. I heard it was comforting, and it makes me feel wonderful that Mark was able to feel much love, prayer, and support in his dying hours.

Back in Hawaii, after learning about Mark, Hannah wanted to leave the beach. We packed up all our stuff and drove a quiet ride back to our timeshare. I just wanted to go back to our timeshare and lay down, but Hannah wanted to be with her cousins so she went to their timeshare. It was what she needed, and I knew she would be well taken care of.

I walked the long steps up to our timeshare. Everything seemed heavy now. I got to our door to find my dad standing outside with tears in his eyes. He had stayed back while we had gone to the beach. When I saw my dad, I knew someone had made sure he was informed. I fell into his arms and sobbed.

I don't remember much about that night. Hannah came back to our timeshare with her cousin, Adelaide, to have a sleepover. She wanted to be with me, but she wanted more support and comfort. I didn't sleep much that night. I expected a call or a text during the night, but it never came.

When I still hadn't gotten the call the next morning, I didn't feel like doing anything. I also knew Hannah needed to do something to keep her mind off of what was going on. Fortunately, she was satisfied with hanging out with her cousins and was okay with me staying back for the day and waiting for "the call". My dad stayed back with me, so I wouldn't be alone.

I couldn't eat. I didn't want to sit out on the deck and look at the sun and beautiful scenery. The palm trees dancing in the wind were hard to take in. At this time, Hawaii's atmosphere was nothing but a nightmare to me. I hated that it was sunny and beautiful. I wanted it to be raining.

I spent a lot of time during the day napping. When I was napping, I didn't have to think. I didn't have to hurt. My mind didn't have to focus on what was going on in my world. But then every time I woke up, reality hit, and I started crying again.

I hadn't gotten a call all day. In the afternoon, I told my dad I needed to get out. I didn't care where, but I needed something different. I wasn't in the mood to go shopping or anything. I felt bad for my dad. He would suggest things, and I would tell him I wasn't in the mood. Finally, we decided on a Dairy Queen trip. I hadn't eaten much all day, but maybe I could somehow swallow an Orange Julius around the lump in my throat.

On September 19, 2019, I posted one of the hardest posts I've ever had to post on Facebook:

I have held off on sharing but I believe it's time. Mark doesn't have much time left on Earth. We were told 24 hours ago that he had 3-5 hours left. In typical Mark fashion, he is a fighter, beating the odds and still with us. But he is fading.

We know God's timing is perfect. We may not like it, but He doesn't make mistakes. My heart told me before we left that something may happen. Mark and I had a conversation about scenarios we could think of. One thing he specifically told me that if he dies, stay in Hawaii. He didn't want us to come home. He also has said many times he didn't want Hannah to watch him die.

As hard as it is to be so far away, we are honoring his wishes. I have been able to talk and FaceTime with him and knowing God led us to have a conversation about this right before we left gives me comfort that I am doing what Mark wants.

That said, being so away is beyond torture. My heart is breaking not only for myself but for my family who love Mark and are so sad, but yet being strong for Hannah and I and doing their very best to keep Hannah busy.

Specific prayers: For Mark to be comfortable as he transitions to his heavenly home and pain-free which I am so grateful for. For Hannah as she is overwhelmed and this is so hard on her. For me as overall I am struggling with so many emotions. For the family as we are saying goodbye to a wonderful man

God's timing is perfect. He knew what Mark wanted, and God is granting his wishes. That gives me some comfort in a very hard time.

God is good and He is with Mark. Soon Mark will be pain- free and see God face-to-face. There are so many emotions right now but we know God is here

Thank you for your thoughts and prayers during this difficult time.

I didn't get a call that day. Mark was still hanging in there. I was relieved as the day kept moving forward without a call as I knew there was likely a good chance then that he wouldn't pass on Peter's birthday.

Another day had passed without "the call".

Mark was still with us the next day. The medical team couldn't believe he was still here and were surprised. I wasn't. Mark was the toughest guy I knew. He was living up to his nickname, the Energizer Bunny.

I kept hearing from those back home that he was resting peacefully and comfortable. It was what I wanted and needed to hear. I don't think I had been able to say that for fifteen years.

There is no way to describe the agony we were in. But I focused on the fact that God was in control. None of this was a surprise to Him, and He was taking care of Mark. Mark couldn't be in better hands. God knew the day Mark would be born and the day Mark would die. I needed to trust in Him and His timing. Easy to say, but not always easy to do.

I was anxious, terrified, and relieved that we were returning home the next day. We would be leaving Hawaii at 8 p.m. With the time changes and layover, we would be getting back to to our house in Wisconsin about 4 p.m. the next day. Such a long day in more ways than one.

Our last day in Hawaii. It wasn't easy, but we made sure to take a beautiful picture with us smiling. I told myself I could force one smile even though it took more energy than I thought I had. My eyes were puffy and nose sore from crying so much. My body hurt from shaking. Hannah wanted a beautiful flower in her hair to show how beautiful Hawaii is. Our world was crashing, but we wanted to show the world how strong and determined we were. We were going to make it together.

We had a layover in Seattle. The flight from Honolulu to Seattle was overnight and long. Many passengers were sleeping. I was especially relieved Hannah was able to sleep. I couldn't sleep though. I couldn't read either. My mind was racing. All I could think about was getting home. I was praying Mark would still be alive so I could see him, talk to him, and give him hugs and kisses. A few days ago, I had been praying that he pass away before we got home. I wasn't sure if I would be able to handle seeing him in the state he was in. But now, it was all I could think about. I needed to get home. I needed to see and touch him one last time. I was worried he would pass while we were on the flight, and no one could get a hold of me.

In Seattle, we had about a three-hour layover at 5 a.m. I had gotten word that Mark was still alive and hanging in there. I was exhausted physically, mentally, and emotionally. Knowing someone could get a hold of me if needed and knowing that at least for the time-being Mark was still alive, I felt I could rest. I was exhausted. I sprawled out on the hard floor of the airport. I didn't care.

It wasn't too long before a stranger poked me in the shoulder and offered me her pillow and blanket. I had tears in my eyes and said, "Thank you so much." This stranger had no idea what I was going through. She didn't know what was ahead for me. I never told her either. I couldn't talk about it. But because of that pillow and blanket, and the kindness of a stranger, I was able to get a good hour of rest. A pillow and blanket never felt so good. I'm sure I'll never meet that woman again. I'm sure she didn't know how much that pillow and blanket meant to me. Some day I hope she will. All she knew at that time was that I would be more comfortable with a pillow and a blanket, and she had an extra one to share.

She was my angel that day. I'll never forget her.

When we finally reached the airport at Minneapolis, we still had just over an hour to drive before getting to our house. Time went so slow and yet so fast. Our house was a couple blocks from the nursing home where Mark was at. We had it all planned so once we got to our house, my mom and I could go immediately to the nursing home. The others would take care of everything else. My family is amazing in times of emergency. We all come together to help each other.

For the first time in a week I was separated from Hannah. She went to April's house so I could be with Mark. She didn't want to see her dad. She was terrified of what she would see. Knowing he was dying was sad and scary for her. I knew I needed to support her. I was worried that one day she would regret not being by her dad's side, but I knew at the time she needed to do what was best for her and not what others thought was best. She was a seven-year-old child dealing with adult circumstances. I didn't want to force her to do something she didn't want to do. To this day, I'm glad she didn't come. I knew it would have been too hard for her. Mark never would have wanted her to see him in the condition he was in. Saying goodbye to her, knowing the next time I would see her I would have to tell her that her daddy died, was excruciating.

I remember every step walking into that nursing home. I wanted to rush in, but at the same time, I wanted to run away. My feet and legs were on auto pilot. They felt like Jell-O. It seemed like walking in took forever. Yet, in the blink of an eye, we arrived at his room.

I'll never forget what I saw when I walked into the room. The guy laying in bed wasn't my Mark. He was so thin. He hadn't eaten or drank for about a week. He was incredibly pale. I couldn't believe he was still here. His eyes were glazed over. There was the awful death smell. The deafening death rattle when he took a breath. The sight, smell, and sounds are things I'll never forget.

It was all too much. Yet, I knew I couldn't break down. I had to be strong for Mark. He had waited for me. The least I could do was be there for him and support him. I had cried enough in front of Mark to know when I cried he focused on me and gave me support. When I hugged him and supported him while he cried, he calmed down. I knew he needed me to be strong. So I touched his hair and cheek, gave him a kiss and said, "I'm here honey. I'm right here. I'm so sorry I was gone but I'm here now."

I'll never forget looking at him for the first time that day. It was the hardest thing I've ever had to do. All I wanted to do was cry and scream. But I held his hand, wiped his forehead of sweat, and kept telling him I was here.

I didn't know what else to say. I was choked up and struggling with words. What do you say to your husband of almost nineteen years whom you know is dying?

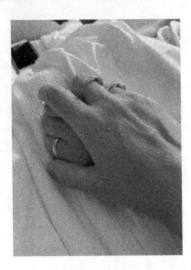

Holding Mark's hand

It was a long night. We had just gotten off the plane from Hawaii. I had little to no sleep in twenty-four hours. Jet lag, five-hour time difference. Emotionally drained to the max.

At about 10 p.m., he was showing signs that his death would be literally any minute. We were certain it was moments away.

But then I saw something shift in his eyes. April, who had been there with him since the beginning of this, said she hadn't seen anything like that type of response all week. Maybe he was looking for me, trying to tell me something, or maybe he saw Jesus. Something was going on. I saw light and movement in his eyes. I couldn't help the tears at that point. I kept telling him I love him, I always would, and I was so proud of him. We put pictures of Hannah to his face. We didn't know if he could see them, but this was the most responsive he had been in a week. We wanted to make sure we took advantage of that and showed him the picture of his precious girl.

That moment didn't last long, but it lasted long enough to know something was there or something was happening. He either wanted to tell me some last words, or he was seeing something incredible. It really doesn't matter. It only matters that the three of us were there (April, my mom, and me). Especially over the past few years, these were the people who were there for Mark the most. It was fitting that we were the ones with him at the end.

By 11:30 p.m., he was still hanging on. It was typical of Mark. April left as she had to be to work in the morning. My mom and I were exhausted from traveling all day, so we decided to lay down. My mom laid on the couch in the room, and I crawled in bed with Mark. I wanted to be as close to him as possible. I laid on just a few inches of the bed, but I was too worried about hurting or squeezing against him. After half an hour, I got out of the bed and slept in a chair next to him. I held his hand the whole time. I was exhausted and even though I didn't want to, I would doze off sometimes. When I woke up, I would whisper to him that I was there and I love him.

I could hear him breathing—a loud raspy breath. A sound you don't forget.

At 2:45 a.m., I realized I couldn't hear the breathing anymore. I called for my mom, and she came running over. I knew in my heart he had passed away. We called for the nurse, and I told her I thought he had passed. She put the stethoscope to his heart and listened. She gave a simple nod.

I hugged and kissed him for the final time as I cried. Death felt real and final. After a few minutes, I stopped touching him altogether. I didn't want to be touching him when his body started getting cold.

My mom and I made the necessary phone calls. Then we waited for the hospice nurse to come and take care of the next steps. My dad came down to be with us, and I was glad he was there. He gave me a hug and then went by Mark's side. There was some silence. Then he said what my mom and I were both thinking.

"You know, I'm kind of jealous of Mark."

I breathed a sigh of relief that the words had been spoken. We talked about how Mark no longer had pain. He had had pain for as long as we had known him, sometimes severe pain. Finally, he had absolutely no pain at all. He had no worries. His eyesight had been poor for a long time and now he could see every single detail. I knew that was something he was looking forward to. He was no longer the one who couldn't see. Technically now we were the "blind" ones. He was in Heaven. He was in pure paradise. This was a paradise far greater than the earthly Hawaiian paradise we had just experienced. This was freedom. This was wholeness. This was the presence of Jesus, and the completion of Mark's suffering and striving.

We all wanted to be there with him.

It's hard to explain how you can be incredibly happy and profoundly sad at the same time. I was already feeling a huge hole tear open in my heart. I missed my husband deeply already. I wanted him back. I wasn't sure how I could keep going because I was devastated. At the same time, I had never felt such joy for Mark. I knew he was looking forward to Heaven. We had talked about it months before. I had said to him, "Mark, do you realize when you're in Heaven, you will have absolutely no pain? And you'll be able to see perfectly!" He looked at me and said, "I just can't imagine that." It gave me tremendous comfort to know he was now experiencing what he couldn't fathom in his wildest dreams. At Mark's funeral, I knew it would only be fitting that the song "I Can Only Imagine" be played. The significance of that song was deeply felt by everyone there.

After the nurse came and talked with us, it was about 4:30 a.m. We could stay with Mark as long as we wanted. We could be there when the funeral home came to get the body. I didn't want to see him being covered up and wheeled out. So just as the funeral home arrived, my parents and I left the nursing home. It was the hardest thing I've ever had to do.

This wasn't the plan Mark and I made. We were supposed to come home from Hawaii and come straight to the nursing home. We would give Mark huge hugs and kisses. His eyes would light up. He would flash his big smile at us like he always did when we got back from a trip. We would pack up Mark's stuff, or knowing him, he would have already had it all packed up and be ready to get out of there. We would get a wheelchair. The nurses would all come in to say bye to Mark and give him a bad time about how much trouble he was. Hannah would wheel him out to the car, and he would get in. Then we would go to our house. I would help Mark into the house and Hannah would talk his ear off while I brought in all the suitcases and bags from Hawaii, dreading the loads of laundry in my future.

That was what was supposed to happen.

Instead, I was walking out of the nursing home with my parents. I was walking further and further away from Mark. All I wanted to do was run back to his room and take him home. There had to be a mistake. There was no way I was leaving without him. With every step, it became harder to move, and my feet became more heavy.

Walking out the door was nauseating. The sun was just coming up. It was a beautiful day. But everything seemed completely different. I couldn't understand why the sun would be shining. Why was the world going forward as if nothing had happened? My first breath outside the nursing home was different. The trees blowing in the wind were different. When I got to my car to open the door, it was like I was on auto pilot. That door was incredibly heavy. I couldn't understand how I was able to open it and then close it. I remember sitting in my car and telling myself I needed to go back in and get him. I couldn't just leave him here. He had to be waking up soon. This was just a big mistake. After all, this was Mark. He *always* pulled through.

I felt like I was going crazy. I knew Mark was gone, but I was having trouble accepting it.

I went to April's house where Hannah was staying. I crawled into bed. I don't even remember if I slept or not. I was in a complete daze.

Hannah woke up after a few hours. When she saw I was there at the house, she knew. I still had to speak the words. I had to tell her that her dad was in Heaven. How was I going to do this? I was going to tell my baby girl awful news. I was supposed to be the one to protect her, not hurt her.

133

I said a quick prayer to God to give me the words. I knew He would, just as He had in Hawaii when I had to tell her that her dad was dying.

As Hannah rubbed the sleep out of her eyes, I bent down to her so we were face-to-face and told her that her dad died. There were no tears and really no reaction except a small nod. I think she was kind of relieved that it had finally happened, and she didn't have to worry about it happening anymore. She looked at me and said, "I really don't want to talk about it. I just want to snuggle with Claire." As much as I was craving to comfort my baby girl, I knew she was seeking the best source of comfort she could tolerate. I was going to do whatever I could to help her through this even if it meant watching her snuggle with her babysitter rather than me. I trusted her judgment of what she needed, and I trusted Claire to provide that support. And I trusted God to get us through this nightmare. It was a lot of trust for such a devastating moment.

The next few days were a whirlwind of activity getting ready for the funeral, meeting with the funeral director and pastor. Mark and I had prepared his funeral months ago. We knew chances were pretty high that I would be planning a funeral for him and not vice versa. He helped me write the obituary and chose songs for his funeral. It wasn't easy to do, but I was relieved we did it then. I was not in the right mindset to make decisions like that now. I think God knew that, so it was one of the things He laid on our hearts to do beforehand.

Hannah had asked me shortly after Mark passed if she would have to go to the funeral. While I knew a lot of people would want to see her, comfort her, and be there for her, I knew going would be too tough for her. I told her that she didn't have to go if she didn't want to. I said we would record the service for her so she could see it later if she wanted to. At that point, it wasn't about what was best for other people but what was best for Hannah. I knew going to the funeral would be too hard for her.

We knew Hannah needed closure and a way to face the reality

of Mark's death. So April designed a "kid friendly" funeral to help her with the loss of her dad. Her closest friends, who had met her dad, all got together, drew pictures, ate orange sherbet like her dad ate when his sugar was low, and released balloons in memory of Hannah's dad. It was good for Hannah and healing for her. I know it helped comfort her in a way she needed and could handle.

✦✦✦✦✦

Looking back, it is evident that God's hand was all over Mark's homecoming. It sounds strange to call a death "beautiful", but Mark's truly was. There are times I wonder if I did the right thing by staying in Hawaii and wonder if I should have come home. But I'm quickly reminded at how perfectly everything turned out, and God planned it just the way it was supposed to be.

There were three things Mark requested when he died: That he see all his brothers and sister one last time, that he was not alone, and Hannah not witness his death. God granted all his requests.

God knew Mark would pass away on September 23, 2019. He also knew Hannah and I would be spending a week in Hawaii during his last days. He had it all planned out. There was a reason the only week we could book with the timeshare was that week. Every detail was perfectly covered by God even though at those moments, it was really hard to see.

In early 2020, a worldwide pandemic hit. Covid-19 became a household name. Everyone stayed home. Nursing homes shut down. Hospitals shut down. Elderly and sick people were dying without their loved ones by their side. People waited in parking lots for news of their loved ones who were in the ER because they couldn't go in with them due to the pandemic. People were dying alone. People couldn't see their loved ones. People were getting bad news and couldn't get comfort from their family and loved ones who could support them the best.

My friend couldn't see a family member struggling with

dementia in the hospital. She was worried he would be wondering why people weren't with him or visiting him. I was grateful I didn't have to experience that with Mark. I cried for their pain. I couldn't imagine. I was relieved I didn't have to live that nightmare. I truly felt blessed that I didn't even have to think about Covid-19. There was comfort knowing I was able to say goodbye to Mark with no limitations. I was able to hold him in my arms at the end of his life. I will forever be grateful that our family was protected from that devastation.

God protected us from that nightmare.

I can't imagine what life would have been like for us if Mark was living during the pandemic and he was in a nursing home. We wouldn't be able to see him. We would have to wave at him through windows and talk with him on the phone. I can picture Hannah's face pressed next to the window, tears running down her cheeks, saying, "I love you Dad!" Mark would be waving back at her saying, "I love you too sweetheart!" He would do his best to put on that beautiful smile of his even though his heart was breaking. After saying goodbye, we would walk away, Hannah crying and leaning into me as I put my arm around her shoulders. She would tell me how much she missed her dad. It would have been hard for all three of us. We would have been fearful of Mark getting Covid-19, suffering alone, not seeing his siblings, children or wife, and dying alone.

Or let's say he was still at home. He would have been considered very high risk, and therefore none of us would have been able to leave the house. No play dates for Hannah. We would be strictly in the house at all times and maybe have to be in separate rooms than Mark. I can imagine there would have been angry feelings and resentment, and living arrangements would be extra hard. God knew 2020 would be a hard year for this world, and He protected us from what would have been a really tough year for all three of us.

As much as I miss Mark, I realize God really did protect all of us. Mark is sitting in Heaven pain-free, perfect eyesight, perfect health, and he has met Jesus. He is free! He is able to watch his daughter have the time of her life with many of her friends. That was something he seldom got to see, and now he has the best seat in the house. I can't think of anything better.

God always provides, and He is good all the time.

CHAPTER 15

SWIMMING WITH THE DOLPHINS

When people look at this picture, they see two people doing something people only dream of in one of the most beautiful places in the world, Hawaii.

When I see this picture, I see two people who just hours before had their world turned upside down. That morning I got the devastating call and had to tell our seven-year-old daughter that her dad was going to die.

If it weren't for Hannah, I would have canceled swimming with the dolphins. I was no longer excited for it at all. I would have forfeited $600, and not care. But for Hannah's sake, I knew I needed to carry on. I knew that's what Mark would want too. It was another thing I didn't have the mental or emotional strength to do. But, I put on that smile for her. I went through it for her. Inside I was broken. My mind was running a million miles a minute. I wanted to be home with my dying husband. The last place I wanted to be was there. But God had it covered. At that moment, Mark's siblings were there at his side fulfilling one of his dying requests.

I look at this picture often because it reminds me of a time when I pushed through like no other. I was strong. I had to be. I was the mother I needed to be for Hannah and the wife Mark wanted me to be. I did it. It was an incredibly hard thing to do, but I did it. This picture reminds me that if I somehow found the strength to put on a smile after I had been given the worst news and having to tell it to my daughter, I can do anything.

God gave me strength. Without God in my corner, this picture wouldn't be possible. That's the only explanation for that smile on my face.

CHAPTER 16

STRUGGLING WITH GRIEF

Up until now, I've been able to share the factual events. What I've come to realize is that regarding grief, nothing is factual. Nothing runs smoothly. Even this chapter probably comes across as being disjointed!

The truth is, sometimes feelings and thinking don't make logical sense or flow easily on the page. Instead feelings are sporadic, intense, fluid, and irrational. Thoughts are in fragments, and sometimes it's hard to even put two sentences together.

Grief is a journey, an evolving experience that seems to be unique to everyone. That is why I am careful to avoid judging people who grieve. Until you are walking the path of grief, it is hard to conceptualize how it affects everyday life.

I thought I was prepared for when Mark passed away, but I've learned nothing can prepare you for the death of someone close to you.

Life was such a rollercoaster ride when Mark was alive. There were many ups and downs when dealing with his health issues. As terrible as it sounds, there was a part of me that was looking for some relief when Mark passed away. At least the rollercoaster ride would be over. What I didn't realize was that when Mark passed away, I may have gotten off that rollercoaster ride, but I didn't leave the park. I simply got on a different ride that disoriented me in new ways.

For the first couple weeks after Mark passed, it was hard to even function. I worked at my job half days, but even that was hard. My brain felt like it was in a fog. I felt like I needed to work to keep busy, but at the same time, my brain didn't seem to be functioning enough to work. Finding that balance was hard.

It seemed unfair to me that my life had completely changed and turned upside down while others' lives continued as normal. After the funeral, everyone else carried on, went back to work, and lived their own lives. Things would never be the same for Hannah and me. Everything was different. No more pills, shots, schedules, or doctors. We were used to having Mark's music on in the house. He basically had his radio station on all the time. He loved listening to music. It was one thing that helped calm him down when he was struggling with pain. It was too quiet without the music on. Yet, it was too hard emotionally to hear it playing. No matter what, it was hard. Many times Hannah and I felt lost, like we didn't know what to do. We would look at each other like, "What do we do now?"

There was a lot paperwork to do and calls to make. Thankfully, my mom helped me do a lot of it. She drove me around to places, so I wouldn't be alone. Errands were exhausting. Thinking and planning, driving and shopping, cooking and eating were more than I could handle. I was emotionally and physically exhausted that even lifting my arms took more energy than I had.

Writing Mark's name on the thank you cards after the funeral was another thing that was extremely difficult. You receive thank you cards from other people, but you never think you'll be writing your husband's name on them. It seems surreal when you do.

It was the little things that hurt badly, like seeing his cereal in the cupboard, or seeing the pill drawer and knowing I don't have to organize his weekly medications every Monday, seeing the electric scooters at Walmart that he always used. I would be sitting in church, thinking I have to check on Mark through the camera app on my phone. It shocked me over and over when I realized I didn't have to do that anymore. Talking about Heaven at church was hard for both Hannah and me. In her AWANA class, there was a time she was supposed to draw a picture of what she thought Heaven looked like. She looked at me with those sad eyes and said, "Mom, this is just a little too hard for me to think about right now. Can I just draw some clouds?" Usually Hannah is excited to talk about Heaven and think about it. Heaven is wonderful. But when you just lost your husband and dad, it can be hard to think about.

I couldn't bear to open the closet or his dresser drawers because I was afraid his scent would leave. I knew eventually it would, and I was scared of losing it.

Hannah was the only reason I got up some mornings. Without her I don't know if I would have been able to do it. I heard from some people how it had to be "so hard to be strong for her" when I was grieving myself. Honestly, being strong for her was the reason I was able to keep going some days. I didn't have a choice.

Everywhere I went it seemed there were couples. I thought to myself, "I hope they know how lucky they are to have each other and I hope they cherish each other."

Time kept moving forward. In some ways it felt like time was flying by and in other ways, it seemed like it was ticking by slowly. Nights were the worst. For years I struggled to sleep because Mark suffered the most at night with severe pain. Some nights he would scream in pain for hours, and that is hard to hear while trying to sleep. I always dreaded nights when Mark was alive. After he passed, I dreaded them for a different reason. Now it was too quiet and I couldn't sleep. I wanted to sleep because when I slept, I didn't hurt. It was the only time when I didn't have to feel my sadness.

His medications and shot stuff were no longer spread everywhere in the house. His clothes weren't in the laundry anymore. His walker no longer was taking up space in the living room. Life seemed like a bad nightmare that I would wake up from. I would pinch myself sometimes to make sure my life was real. Everything was different.

Even the way the sun shone during the day seemed much different. The air I breathed felt different. I didn't like that it had all changed. Every day my mind would try to wander back to what I knew was normal, but then quickly reminded myself that it isn't my normal anymore. "Normal" took on a whole new meaning.

For years, I was constantly on edge listening for Mark and helping Mark. I was always listening for his voice or movement in case he needed me. It was exhausting. But I also kept reminding myself one day I would have all the rest time and "me" time I want, and I should cherish the exhaustion and time with Mark. While I certainly tried, I admit I wasn't the best at cherishing it enough. When he passed, I had a lot of quiet and rest time and "me" time. People imagined I would love that change. But the constant stillness and quiet left a depression few understood. I felt lost.

———————— ✦✦✦✦✦ ————————

About a month after Mark had passed, someone asked me if Mark's death was easier on me because I knew it was coming. The question caught me off guard. Easier than what? I told this person we definitely didn't expect to go to Hawaii and then come home only having a few hours left with Mark. He was on hospice, but we also knew hospice didn't necessarily mean "end of life". He did have a lot of health issues and we knew we would most likely be dealing with his death sooner rather than later at some point. It wasn't "easier" just because I knew it would be coming. His death was hard, and honestly nothing could make it easier. There was some comfort knowing he wouldn't be suffering anymore, but even having that knowledge didn't make my heart hurt any less.

I heard other well-meaning comments too. I know people meant well, but they were hard to hear. People would say, "At least with Mark on hospice, you had time to prepare" and "He's finally out of pain so it's hard to be real sad." It made me question my feelings. Was I grieving "too much"? Was I not entitled to feel as sad as I did?

Shortly after Mark passed, I talked with someone who lost their husband suddenly. I couldn't imagine the shock of my husband gone in an instant. I told her my heart broke for her. I couldn't imagine how she was feeling. She told me she couldn't imagine what I was going through—-years of watching my husband suffer like he did. It made me realize any death is hard and hurts more than you ever can imagine or "prepare" for. It doesn't matter how it happens. Death is just plain hard. It's not fair. I feel like I've been cheated out of a life with a healthy husband, he was cheated out of watching Hannah grow up, and Hannah has been cheated out of having her dad with her.

I don't know that watching your husband suffer for years or losing your husband suddenly can even be compared. Losing a spouse either way is torture, even when you know they are in Heaven. You long for your love back, to be hugged again, to be kissed, to have your best friend there. I married Mark knowing he was sick, knowing I would not have a long marriage or celebrate a fiftieth wedding anniversary. I thought I knew what I was getting into, although I never guessed the extent of heartache I'd experience. We were married 18-1/2 years. That is it. There are no more anniversaries to celebrate. It's like a wall was erected on our marriage timeline.

I assume my grief is different than someone who loses someone suddenly and unexpected. I didn't experience the complete shock of losing a healthy partner. I also take comfort in knowing I had the chance to say what I needed to say before Mark passed. On the other hand, I also watched Mark suffer for years. I spent years in and out of the hospital. I lost out on many "normal" marriage experiences. Every grief is different, and I believe every grief is hard.

I also married Mark knowing that we serve an awesome God. A God who actively performs miracles. Even though the miracle I prayed for desperately was for Mark to be completely healed, God did perform miracles in other ways. Mark's life was full of miracles. When I look back, I'm incredibly grateful for them. I prayed many times for Mark to be healed. He was healed, just not in the way I had envisioned.

I anticipated I would be a widow. We were married knowing that Mark's health indicated we wouldn't be married for a long time. I had thought five years would be a gift but we made it over eighteen years! We had planned his funeral together. Mark made sure home improvements were done so I wouldn't have to worry about it. We knew exactly how much our finances would be impacted when Mark passed. Mark wanted to know we would survive without him. We certainly didn't have the perfect marriage and had plenty of disagreements. We also didn't hold back telling each other how much we loved each other because we didn't know when it would be the last time those words would be spoken.

Even though I knew Mark was sick, I loved him and married him. I knew Mark was in hospice, was critically ill, and I still longed for a miraculous healing. Sometimes I wonder if I am entitled to still grieve and be sad. I'm not sad he is in Heaven. I'm not sad he isn't in pain anymore. I'm not sad I don't have to deal with doctors, medications, and the fear of not knowing what each day will bring. But I am sad because I miss Mark. I miss seeing him. I miss everything about him. You can be as prepared as well as you think you can be, but you can never prepare your heart for the pain of never seeing your spouse, the one you've been with nearly all the time, day and night, for almost nineteen years, every day.

———— ♦♦♦♦♦ ————

Two months after Mark passed, the holiday season was upon us. Throughout our marriage, I had always wrapped the Christmas presents. For the most part I enjoyed it, and it was too hard for Mark to help. When I wrapped them, I would wrap them while Mark rested on the couch and watched me. We would talk about what we got people. Sometimes Mark had no idea what presents we had gotten people so I would show him what "we" got. I think everyone who is married knows what I'm talking about. The wife's Christmas shopping list is a mile long for gifts to get while the husband's Christmas shopping list is pretty short. Mark's list was: Tammy. I didn't realize how much that time meant to me and how precious it was until I was wrapping Christmas presents the year Mark passed. The couch was empty, and I had no one to talk to.

The first holiday season after Mark passed was hard. My family, friends, and church family were determined to make Christmas special, especially for Hannah. Our church family surprised us with boxes of gifts and an L.O.L. Ice Chalet for Hannah. This was a big ticket item that she wanted. It was too expensive for me to get it for her. I felt amazingly blessed. A sweet friend told me that Christmas, "You have a lot to be sad about this holiday season, but also a lot to be happy about." Such true words.

The holidays were tough for sure, but I found the times that popped up unexpectedly were the worst. Those "everyday moments" come up completely out of the blue and without warning.

For example, Mark always watched the weather and news like a hawk. I didn't. The news was always too depressing. I really didn't need to worry about what was going on. Mark told me the big things going on in the world, and I depended on him for weather reports. He would tell me about weather that would impact my driving or Hannah's school. The first snow storm we got after he passed that everyone else knew was coming except me because I didn't watch the news hit me so hard that I was in the fetal position on the floor crying. Finding an old test strip while cleaning can make me burst into tears. Hearing "his" radio station over the loudspeaker in Walmart could make me cry in the middle of a store and in front of everyone. Anniversaries are tough. Holidays are tough. Sometimes everyday moments are even tougher. I learned to be kind always. That stranger who was rude to you may be having an everyday moment that is too hard to handle. Everyone needs to share and show love because you have no idea what anyone is going through at any given moment.

--------------------◆◆◆◆◆◆--------------------

There are times I think back to our old life and I'm hit with the reality that that life is over. For example, there are times I think to myself "I need to make a lab appointment for Mark." Then it hits me that I don't have to do that anymore. I catch myself wondering why the pharmacy isn't calling to set up our monthly medication order. Then it hits me that they won't be calling anymore. Sometimes I feel panicky when I see the house is dark and no lights are on when I'm driving home at night. I have to remind myself that there is no one in the house to need the lights on. I drive by the hospital and think to myself how lucky we are that we haven't been there in awhile. I wonder when he will be in there again only to remember he isn't here anymore to need the hospital.

Some mornings I wake up and think to myself, "Mark can't really be gone, can he? This just could not have happened. I can't really be a widow, can I? There has to be some mistake." Then reality hits, and it's like losing him all over again.

Reality can be cruel at times.

As I adjust to this reality, I notice many things that trigger tears. I see people walking with walkers and start to cry. I see people drop off patients at the front of the clinic and I cry. I drive past the nursing home where Mark passed away at least twice a day to bring Hannah back and forth to school. Every time I drive by there I think of those last few days of his life. Sometimes it seems like I just walked out of those doors and sometimes it feels like an eternity has passed. I remember walking out of those doors on a beautiful morning when he died. I relive that horrible day every time I drive past. I hate sunny mornings because it reminds me of the morning I had to say goodbye. Rainy days are much easier than sunny days.

One of the biggest adjustments for me was going from being

needed as a caregiver twenty-four hours a day, seven days a week to not being needed at all. I know Hannah needed me but it was a different way. She still had a lot of the same things going on in her life that hadn't changed—school, friends, sports. She could get dressed herself, brush her teeth and hair, shower, etc. For almost nineteen years, Mark depended on me all the time. Sometimes he needed me for even the littlest things like getting up from a chair or getting things from a shelf. We would go to bed every night not knowing if he would get any sleep without me managing pain medications for him. I was constantly on edge just in case he needed me to help him get up to go to the bathroom as he couldn't see in the dark and had trouble walking. When Mark was alive, it took a lot of planning to schedule help and assistance for me to be able to leave town for a day or two with Hannah. It was almost easier to stay home.

Now that Mark wasn't here anymore, I didn't know what my purpose was. I was always Mark's wife. His schedule always dictated my schedule. I was always limited on what I could do because I needed to be there for him. While it was stressful and demanding, I was needed. It was all on my shoulders, but I knew my purpose was to be there for him and love Mark.

Now things were different. No appointments to be made. No driving him to places. No calls to hospice. Nothing. I hated different. I was no longer multi-tasking. My workload was suddenly cut drastically. I struggled to adopt to the sudden overwhelming abundance of time. I didn't know how to fill the minutes during the day, much less the hours and days.

I felt helpless. Everyone kept telling me that I still had a purpose. I knew in my heart it was true. I wouldn't be here if I didn't have a purpose. God had me here for a purpose. But I felt different. I knew Hannah needed me, but I also knew she was perfectly happy playing with her friends, and she wasn't dependent on me. A lot of the time she would come home for a few minutes and then announce she was leaving to go play with her friends.

I was by myself a lot. It was a huge change. I transitioned from never having a minute alone to always being alone. When Mark was alive, I craved just thirty minutes to read a book with a cup of coffee. Now I had time, but what I really wanted was to be needed again, to find my purpose, and to find me.

"What do you like to do?" is a question that is an easy one for most people to answer. But after Mark passed, I didn't know how to answer that. I now struggle with my identity. I don't even know what I really like to do anymore. My life had been focused on growing up, attending college, getting married, and becoming a caregiver. Forty-four years of focusing on what I needed to do to work toward a goal. Caring for Mark and Hannah became my life's purpose! Now I feel alone and lost. I wonder where do I go from here?

Over the last few years, when I was exhausted from being a caregiver and a mom, I promised myself one day I would have all the time in the world for me. Mark would be in Heaven, and Hannah would be busy with friends. I could rest then. I needed to enjoy time with Mark and Hannah now. Even though I was burned out from exhaustion, I knew one day I would wish for it back. I've definitely found that to be true. I now had lots of quiet and "me" time, and I just didn't know what to do with it.

Being a caregiver is harder than anyone realizes unless you have been through it. I'd do it all over again. It was a tough and exhausting road. If anyone is a caregiver and in the position I was, please know you aren't alone, even though you feel lonely. I was a caregiver for almost nineteen years. Right now, I'm trying to cherish the time I have with Hannah. Take vacations and not worry about work or money. Time with Hannah is much more important.

Most of all, put God first. Pray and He will show me what He wants me to do now. He knows my identity better than me. Trust in Him, and the rest will fall into place.

✦✦✦✦

I booked a cruise in the summer of 2019 (before Mark had passed) for February 2020. I had felt guilty booking it. In typical Mark fashion, he had encouraged Hannah and me to go. I was looking forward to it for months. I wanted to let loose with some friends and have a really good time.

I was surprised at my tumultuous emotions before heading out on that trip. Talk about a roller coaster. When Mark was alive, before leaving on a trip, big or small, there was always a lot of stress, scheduling stuff for Mark, finding people to check in on him, etc. I remember I craved the day I would just have to worry about Hannah and me. Now, that that time had come, I felt guilty for having to just worry about Hannah and me. I felt guilt, then excitement, then sadness. It was really not how I imagined I'd feel when I booked it.

I had come to realize "firsts" were not only for positive things like holidays and trips, but also negative things like not having to go crazy with planning cares for Mark. No scheduling people to come visit with Mark, bring him meals, line up hospice nurses, get pills all sorted out with a timer so he knew when to take them, etc.

Getting ready for the cruise was easy. There was virtually nothing to do but pack. It was just Hannah and me to worry about. It was different now, and that made me sad. It really caught me off guard. I couldn't figure out why I was feeling depressed. Then I realized that this was another "first"—first time leaving for a long trip without having to worry about Mark. There were also times on the cruise it would hit me that I didn't have to check on him, and it was hard.

I was also not prepared for the grief I felt when we came home. Getting off the ship, my friends all had husbands to call to let them know we were back on land. They were eager to share stories, but I didn't have anyone to tell. That was hard. Mark was always at home waiting for us after a trip, usually opening up the door for us. It didn't matter what time of the day or night we got home, he would be waiting for us. I would tell him not to, but he was stubborn. He would be excited to see us and give us hugs. He would want to know all about it. Coming home to a dark house and not having Mark to welcome us was hard after that trip.

✦✦✦✦✦

2019 was a hard year of losses for me. I lost the love of my life, two close friends, five friends/supporters who were always there for Mark and me, and one of my dear friends lost her husband only two weeks after Mark passed away. I told people that 2019 was a terrible year for Earth, but what an amazing year for Heaven. I couldn't help but smile when I thought of the party that had to be going on up there. The losses I experienced saved many people much stress and heartache. People who suffered health issues didn't have to go through the Covid-19 pandemic. What a blessing for them.

2020 was a hard year for anyone struggling with grief. Every day I thank God that He protected Mark from Covid-19. God protected our whole family. We could have been living a nightmare, and I'm glad Mark didn't have to feel the fear and anxiety that many felt.

But selfishly, for me, the isolation wasn't easy. It was lonely. When the pandemic hit, I was just coming up on the six-month anniversary of Mark's death which I had been told was a hard anniversary. Reality seemed to hit at that time, and I was preparing myself for it as much as I could. But I hadn't prepared for the pandemic occurring. We had to stay at home and we were constantly reminded Mark wasn't here. Many of us struggling with grief depend on distractions to keep busy and our mind off of missing our loved ones. During the Covid-19 pandemic shut downs, our support groups weren't able to meet in person. We couldn't go to work. We couldn't go to the movies, go bowling, or a casual shopping trip with girlfriends. Our options were limited. We were lonely as it was, but the "stay-at-home" rules magnified the loneliness and depression.

Of course I leaned on God and trusted Him. God is a wonderful Protector. He protected our family during this tough time, and I was grateful. But it was still hard. We were sad. We were lonely. We needed our friends and family. I realized just how much I've *needed* to do things and have distractions, not just that I *wanted* them. Keeping busy kept my mind busy. Bringing Hannah to church and events helped me think of other things. It was what was healing my heart.

Staying at home with just Hannah and me caused my anxiety to skyrocket. I thought of Mark so much and missed him terribly. I cried every day, usually multiple times a day. I saw my parents from afar occasionally. I couldn't get hugs when I desperately need them. Everything at home reminded me of Mark. I spent my extra time cleaning out stuff at home. I usually found something of his or something that reminded me of him. Doing yard work made me think of how he used to mow the lawn (or when he wasn't able to do it, watch as I did it). Seeing his tools in the garage—his spot— reminded me of the projects he wanted to do when he felt better.

Grief hits me in waves. Sometimes one thing could bring me down that normally wouldn't, and I have no idea when that will happen. Some days are easier to move forward than other days. One minute I can be fine and the next, I am sobbing so hard I can barely breathe. Walking in grief every day is like playing emotional roulette. I never know what kind of emotions I will face that day. I could be doing fine and then go into a complete panic because I have to get the mail. I never know what to expect in the mailbox. Sometimes there are items in there that make me burst into tears.

Some days are so hard they knock me off my feet. It takes a lot just to lift my body off the bed. Getting dressed and brushing my teeth sometimes takes more energy than I have. I feel nauseous, my head pounds, and I worry about the future. How can my life go on? I feel like I can't move.

Eventually I am able to stand up again. It might be in a few minutes or a few days, but it does happen. God has shown to me multiple times in my life that I will survive the most painful, unthinkable agony. I will be okay. I will make it. That is what gets me through the tough days. I know the waves of grief will come, and some days are harder than others. But I also know the waters eventually calm down too. Grief is like an ocean of waves, unpredictable and ever changing.

We always said we didn't want regrets, but I'd be lying if I said I didn't have any. I have moments when I feel a lot of guilt and regret. I replay all the times I hurt Mark and all the times I should have done something different. We endured a lot of stress and pressure in our lives. We were both exhausted and frustrated. At times we both said hurtful things, and we always did apologize. Sometimes all I can focus on is the fact that I hurt him in the past, and I can't say I am sorry again. I think about all the missed time I lost out on with him. I always tried to spend as much time with Mark as I could so I wouldn't have any regrets. I still do feel regret. I think about the times I could have spent with him but I chose to do something else instead. Friday nights were always "my night". I would usually hang out with friends so I could get a break for a few hours. I know I needed the break at the time, but now that he is gone, I wish I wouldn't have left him.

I find myself looking back a lot at all those "what if's" and "should haves". There are things I would have done differently. There are many "why didn't I do this?" or "I wish I would have done this." I knew Mark wouldn't want me to feel this way. He would want me to think of the happy times and not the sad times. He wouldn't want me thinking about the regrets. I knew he wanted me to know I "was an amazing wife and he loved me so much." He would tell me to be strong for Hannah and take care of her. He would want me to think of the good times because we had so many of them. All the laughs. All the times we were picking on each other. All the hugs. We were in love and endured a lot more than other couples. We were strong. I know he desperately wanted me to think of the good times and all the smiles and laughs.

Sometimes I have flashbacks of Mark's last days, and I can't help but think of what I could have done differently. I tried not to cry in front of him so he wasn't scared. I was strong for him, but did that make him think I didn't care because he didn't see me crying? Hannah never saw him when he was dying. He said he didn't want her to see him dying because he was afraid it would traumatize her. But in his last moments, did he really want her there? Was he craving her touch one last time? We had just gotten back from Hawaii. I was exhausted. Between 11:30 p.m. and 2:45 a.m., there were about three hours that I was dozing off and not fully there for him. Did he need me and he couldn't get my attention? Was he scared? Did he try to communicate to me with his eyes, and I was too exhausted to notice? Why didn't I keep laying next to him even if it was hurting him? It was my last chance to feel his body next to mine. He would soon be pain-free anyway. What did he want to say and do in the last hours I was with him? What was he thinking? Did he need something? Hurting? Wanting to tell me something? I find myself replaying everything.

Sometimes I still cry in the shower because I don't have to work to wipe the tears away. They just wash away. Hannah can't hear me sob so I can cry as hard as I want. Showers are sometimes my sanctuary.

✦✦✦✦✦

One of the things that frightened me the most when Mark died was wondering how in the world I was going to help Hannah through it. We tried as best we could to mentally "get ready" since Mark was chronically ill. She started seeing a therapist when Mark was enrolled in hospice. One of my best friends was a child psychologist, so I had wonderful advice and support. But no one ever knows how a child will react and how your state of mind will be during a time of grief.

What I have learned is to let Hannah take the lead. She can make the decision not to attend her dad's funeral services, how to handle holidays and birthdays, and what to do for the annual Daddy/daughter school dance. She is terrified of losing me. She has always been super attached to me, but now it is even more so. I do what I can to make her feel comfortable even if that means calling her when I make it to Walmart so she knows I'm safe.

I have told Hannah, "I have no clue what you're going through because I've never lost a dad, but I promise we will be here for each other. I will always be here to listen and help you through it."

My best advice to other parents of grieving kids is to let the kids take the lead. They know what's best. Don't just do what you think is best or what others say is best. Kids are the best judge of what they need. They are smart. They guide you if you are there for them and listen. That's all they want.

++++++

One of the most comforting statements said after Mark passed was at his funeral when his primary doctor stood up and said, "I was Mark's physician, but really Tammy was his doctor. She was the one who took care of him and she did a great job." Then I watched as he fought tears. Those words meant a lot to me. For nineteen years, I doubted myself. Others doubted me. I would get questions from other people about why he was eating the things he was, why I wasn't taking him into the ER, why I enrolled him in hospice, etc. I was always being questioned, especially the last year of his life. There were times I agreed with his doctor and times I disagreed. We talked so often that I considered him a big brother. We talked to him more than some of our family. In fact, at his funeral Mark insisted he and his family sit with our family because they were family to him. They were there during his last days when I couldn't be.

So when his doctor, the one who talked to and knew Mark the best, said that, he put my fears to rest. I did take good care of him.

Words can truly mean the world to someone. You may not think what you have to say is that big of a deal, but it might just be. I've learned to give people compliments whenever I can. You never know when the words you say may make a huge difference for someone.

Another friend shared these special words with me. "The first time I met Mark, I wondered how he had made it this long. His condition was poor for so long and that was clear. It was his spirit, his resolve, and his support system that kept him going. His body was literally giving out. Yet, he pushed past the pain to keep living and loving his family. I think of him when I see a guy with a little scratch on his leg whining and wailing in pain. I think to myself, you don't know pain! I wish you would have met Mark. Then you'd understand pain and see the resolve to push past it. He loved every moment of life. Without the love and support of his family, he never would have made it nineteen amazing years! Your final act of love was giving him the gift of hospice to give him the comfort and peace his earthly body rarely got to experience. One of our hospice doctors always says, 'Dying is an inevitable place we are all going. With hospice, you get to choose how you'd like to get there-- 1973 Ford Truck or 2020 Cadillac!' He was really lucky to get the Cadillac."

Special words that were comforting to hear. I'll never forget them.

I promised Mark before he died that I would never stop talking about him. I wouldn't let anyone forget him. I'd constantly remind people of how he inspired others and how God worked many miracles in his life. Mark kind of smirked and told me he couldn't imagine what kind of inspiration he was. He felt guilty he was still living when others who were active in the community would suddenly pass away. He would ask why them and not me? He felt like he didn't have much to give to others.

Mark couldn't see it then, but I'm sure he does now. I'm sure God sat him down and told him just how he has changed the world. I know Mark understands now why he went through everything he did and how the pieces of the puzzle fit together. To him, it all makes sense. I feel great comfort knowing that Mark understands everything. I also believe Mark sees God's plan for Hannah and me. If he could, he'd say, "I know you're sad Tammy, but I can now see the big picture. I promise you it's all for good. I've spoken with God, and it's so cool! I'm so happy for you!" Mark's in a place where he understands much more now than we can. I'm really happy for him.

I often wonder if people expect Christians not to grieve because they know their loved one is in Heaven pain-free and happy. What is there to be sad about when we will see each other again? I've come to realize that I'm sad because I'm human, he's in Heaven, and I'm not with him. It's okay to cry and it's okay to smile. It's okay to wish Mark was here, and it's okay to be grateful he is in Heaven.

It's okay to be angry that I have no more time with Mark here, and it's okay to be thankful for the time I did have with him.

It's okay to just be alone, and it's okay to be with others.

It's okay to say no when I'm not feeling like doing something, and it's okay to say yes when I do feel like it.

It's okay to ignore a phone call or text when I'm not up to talking to someone, and it's okay to pick up the phone when I need to hear from someone.

It's okay to talk about Mark when I want to, and it's okay not to when it hurts too much.

It's okay to feel one emotion one minute and a completely different emotion the next.

Most important I have come to realize that it's okay not to be okay. It's okay to be homesick for Heaven. I have comfort in knowing that even Jesus cried when He heard Lazarus died, and He knew Lazarus would come back to life soon! I know it's okay to cry because I miss Mark. I still miss our time together even though I will see him again. He is in a place I can only imagine the splendor of it. It doesn't make me any less of a Christian because of how I'm feeling. I'm just a lonely wife missing her husband who is no longer physically by my side.

I know better than anyone else how much Mark truly suffered. I don't miss that. I don't miss the screaming. I don't miss the constant testing, schedules, and doctor's appointments (although I DO miss the doctors and nurses). I don't miss the tears. I don't miss the arguments and the stress. There is a lot I don't miss. In fact, I actually feel relieved that part is over.

What do I miss?

I miss his hugs. I miss his smile. I miss when he could just look at me and know what I was thinking. I miss that I could talk to him about anything. I miss that only he knew what I needed. I miss the way his hand rubbed the small of my back. I miss that whenever he would have trouble getting up after he fell, I would ask him to give me a hug, and I'd lift him up that way. His brain injury made him forget a lot of things, but he never forgot how to hug me. I miss that. I miss the way his eyes lit up when he saw Hannah. I miss the way he yelled "Bye sweetheart!" every morning when Hannah left for school. I miss watching him wrestle with Hannah on the couch. I miss those goofy jokes he told that he thought were so funny. I miss how he gave 110 percent no matter what. I miss how he wanted to give to others without expecting something in return. I miss the way he was always there. I miss holding his hand. I miss kissing his cheek. I missing feeling his body next to mine. I miss him calling me "honey". I miss the Mark I knew. Most people knew him as a sick, unfortunate guy who is finally pain-free. I knew Mark as the man who stole my heart and loved me more than anyone ever could. He was my husband, the love of my life and always will be.

That's a lot of missing.

Someone told me when Mark passed away that people are going to tell you it gets easier with time, but that's not actually true. You just learn to deal with it differently. At the time that was discouraging to hear, but I've found those words to be right on the nose. Hearing those words were exactly what I needed to hear.

Grief has been such a journey of learning.

It's still hard to get up in the morning, but I've learned how to do it.

It's still hard to smile when I don't feel like it, but I've learned to make it happen.

It's still hard to hold my daughter as she cries, but I've learned to sit with her in her sorrow.

It's still hard to call myself a widow, but I've learned it's not my whole story.

I will never say to someone who is grieving, "It's been a long time, so it should be getting easier". It's not a long time. Losing someone never "gets easier" per se. It changes you. Grief is the price you pay for loving. To grieve deeply is to know that you loved so much. What a gift. What a blessing.

I never want people to feel sorry for me. I just want to be understood. I want people to "get it". I want people to listen. I want the hugs and hearing, "I'm here for you." A friend read a book on grief during the holidays just so she would know what I was going through the first holiday season after Mark passed. She said to me, "There is so much people don't even realize. I'm so sorry." That meant the world to me that she wanted desperately to understand me and my feelings.

One of the things I'm always repeating to myself, which is most comforting to me, is that this is our temporary home. We're only passing through. One day this will all be behind me, and I will see my husband again.

CHAPTER 17

CLOSING THOUGHTS

I can just imagine what my conversation could've been like with God in May 2001 as I'm getting ready to marry the love of my life.

Mark was not doing well that day. Even though it was our wedding day, he had gone through three hours of dialysis that morning. He was really struggling to get through the day. All of us wanted to put a chair in the front for Mark so he could rest through the ceremony, but he insisted he was fine. My focus that day was not so much our wedding, but trying to get Mark through it and making sure he was okay.

I can imagine my reaction if God had this conversation with me on our wedding day. Just before I'm about to walk down the aisle God says, "Tammy, Mark is very sick. I know you don't think he'll live much longer, but I will make it possible for Mark to receive a kidney transplant. Despite all odds, eighteen years from now, his kidney will still be functioning great. I will answer your prayers, and you will buy a house you love. Not only that, I will give you a daughter who you will name after a woman in the Bible who struggled too. I know you will give glory to Me, and I thank you. I will caution you, the journey to bring her home will be long and hard, but you will have a daughter. You will celebrate eighteen years of marriage before I will take Mark home to be with Me."

I would've rolled my eyes and laughed at His obvious joke.

Yep, I would've laughed at God. I wouldn't have believed my life would turn out the way it did when Mark and I exchanged vows in May 2001. Maybe that is why God didn't tell me all of this at the start. When I look back, I can see God is faithful. He doesn't promise easy roads or life without struggle. God remained faithful throughout our journey. Life is full of blessings I wouldn't have experienced had I not been struggling. These are times that turn us toward God. They teach us lessons that remind us to believe and look for God.

Everyone suffers. There is no question about that. But everyone's suffering is different. From the time we got married in 2001, our suffering stemmed mostly around Mark's diabetes, kidney and heart failure, and endless surgeries. We struggled for eight years with infertility.

I'd love to tell you I've never questioned God's plan. But that is not true. I try to be an upbeat, positive, "glass half-full" type of person, but it doesn't always work out that way. Mark was the same way. I admired him a lot because most of the time he was positive. He didn't question why he had diabetes or blame God. Although, at times he did get furious with the pain.

But one thing I know is that God will use everything for His glory, even suffering. He will allow us to suffer so we reach out to Him. Hannah is a blessing that came after years of suffering. Hannah is God's blessing and a reminder He was aware of our suffering.

It's important to give God the glory. Giving glory to God is a natural response to recognizing divine intervention. When you see God's hand in anything, you are overwhelmed by it all and cannot stop yourself from giving glory to God. Giving glory is another word for engaging in appreciation of God.

As I am writing this, it has been just over two years since Mark has gone to his heavenly home. The first year after he passed was hard, but I think the second year was even harder. In the first year, you are still in a state of shock. In the second year, reality hits. Your loved one is really not coming back.

Even though it has been hard, I have made it. I have survived. I am still here.

For years I've heard, "God will never give you more than you can handle", and for years I believed it. I can tell you it's not true.

Have you ever felt like you just have too much on your plate? You can't possibly add one more thing on there. At times God will fill our plates so full that it is too heavy to carry ourselves. We drop the plate on our foot, and it hurts. It hurts so bad that we cry out to Him. That's what He wants us to do. If the plate hadn't been so full, dropped, landed on your foot, and hurt so much, would you have cried out to Him? No. You would have kept moving forward.

I've looked back at my life, and I can give you examples of when I felt I was at my breaking point. It may not have been a breaking point for others, but it was for me. I've felt I couldn't deal with anything anymore. And you know what I did? I prayed. I cried. I told God I just couldn't do it anymore. I'd get angry at Him for putting me or Mark through so much. I'm ashamed to admit it, but I have gotten extremely angry at God.

Had I not gotten to that breaking point and cried out to Him, I wouldn't have seen God's hand at work. There have been times I've heard the perfect song at the perfect time, and it was what I needed to hear.

I call it a "God thing".

I've asked for prayer from others when things got tough and suddenly things turn around or maybe my heart just calms because I know people are praying.

That is a "God thing".

After miscarrying our embryo babies, I was depressed. I couldn't get out of bed. I was angry and disappointed with God. Through His gentle urging, I got through it. I got out of bed and moved on. That happened only after I simply told Him I couldn't do it without His help.

Another "God thing".

Raising $10,000 almost overnight to bring our baby Hannah home was impossible. I prayed to God to find a way, help us, because I knew only He could do this. God spoke to the hearts of many and people gave generously that exact amount.

You can't call that anything but a "God thing"!

A few years before Mark passed away, I was introduced to a woman whose husband was also struggling with serious medical issues. We both leaned on each other for support while trusting God had His hand in our lives. Our husbands passed away within two weeks of each other. We have daughters around the same age, walking the same grief timeline, and we love God with all our heart. God knew we would need each other for support during our difficult grief journeys both for ourselves and our daughters and He brought us together. He didn't promise life would be without pain, but He did promise He would help us through it. He provided for our families at just the right time.

We call it a "God thing".

God DOES give you more than you can handle so you turn to Him. Just think if things were always peachy and rosy and things fell into our laps without having to work on it or anything. Would we ever reach out to God to help us? Why would we need God's strength? Would we feel like we ever needed God? Maybe we would be thankful, but even thanking God doesn't happen as often as pleading for His help. I know if He didn't give me more than I could handle, I wouldn't have the relationship I have with Him today. I've had trials and tribulations but all of that has drawn me closer to Him. *So that's why it's a God thing.*

And I'm thankful. What a wonderful and gracious Father we have.

I am grateful I have gone through this journey. I've cried oceans, BUT I've smiled more. My faith has been tested, BUT I've learned to trust God more. I've realized He has a plan, and He will always provide. At times there was more stress and strain in our marriage,

BUT it also made us stronger. We learned to lean on each other more. I've met people in my life who I otherwise wouldn't have met. I've realized not everything comes easy, and I take a lot for granted. I've also learned to trust in God's timing. His timing is always perfect even if it means sometimes waiting much longer than we would like.

As hard and painful as this journey has been, I'm humbled God chose me to go through it. I'm honored to share God's works in my life.

My dear Readers,

If you would like to experience Heaven, like Mark is right now, you can! Jesus died on the cross for your sins so you can spend eternity with Him in perfect paradise. It is a free gift. All you have to do is pray this prayer: "Dear Lord, I admit I am a sinner. I have lived my life for myself only. I ask for Your forgiveness. I believe that You died on the cross to save me from my sins. You did what I could not do for myself. I give myself to You. I want You to take control of my life. Help me to live my life in a way that pleases You. I love You. I thank You that I will spend eternity with You. Amen."

I want you to trust and believe God does have a plan for your life, and it is good. It may not feel like it all the time, but He works everything out for our good and for His glory. He performs miracles. Sometimes you must wait, but waiting isn't a bad thing. In my experience, it's meant something better is coming. I know it's hard to be patient and, trust me, there have been many times I have prayed to God to give me patience (God, if you could hurry up with that patience, that would be great.). I also encourage you to look and see how faithful God has been in your life. He is faithful every day, even with things we don't even think about. He is faithful by providing us the rising and setting of the sun, in daylight and darkness. He is faithful in providing us food and nourishment. He is faithful in providing a roof over our heads. Even having a pillow to lay our head on at night is a sign of His faithfulness. I'm sure you can think of many times in your life when He has been faithful and provided for you if you take some time to think of it. Know whatever you are facing right now or will face in the future, He is there. He is faithful. He is trustworthy. He is taking care of you.

Focus on Mark's life as an example of God's presence. Never give up and always smile even when life is tough.

My favorite lesson Mark taught Hannah was when she was complaining about life not being fair. Mark's life was the epitome of unfair. Mark, who suffered from juvenile diabetes. Mark, whose body seemed to rebel at him at every turn. Mark, who faced more suffering and pain than you or I will likely face in our entire lives. He deserved none of the hardship that he lived with, and still his perspective remained in tune with God's goodness and grace in his life.

"Hannah", he said, "Life isn't fair, but life is good."

Tammy and Hannah in July 2021